PERSONAL ACCOUNTABILITY

PERSONAL ACCOUNTABILITY

*Powerful and Practical Ideas
for You and Your Organization*

JOHN G. MILLER

Denver Press

Published by Denver Press
P.O. Box 625
Brighton, CO 80601

ISBN 0-9665832-0-5
Library of Congress Catalog Card Number: 98-96450

Designed by Ciavolino & Sheeler Marketing Communications
Baltimore, Maryland
http://www.cands.com

—————————————————————

Additional copies of *Personal Accountability* are available *exclusively* through Denver Press.
Call 800-681-9827 or order through the internet at www.QBQ.com today.

Dedication

To all those who asked for this book to be written
because they understand the power of Personal Accountability

Contents

Preface

In 1995 I experienced a life-changing moment. I suddenly realized what I wanted to do and be after spending nine years in the corporate training industry as a salesperson, consultant and facilitator. I wanted to become a professional keynote speaker.

I remember the experience vividly. It happened on the Radisson Diamond cruise ship, when my wife, Karen, and I were participating in the President's Council trip—The Fortune Group's annual reward for outstanding achievement. We were attempting to bronze our bodies on deck the first day out of Puerto Rico, when another passenger asked me a pretty standard question.

The nice man in his 60s, wearing a traditional tourist hat, inquired politely, "John, what do you do for a living?"

For nine years I had been answering, "I sell and implement leadership and sales training for corporations."

That day, though, I confidently said, "I am a professional speaker!"

I quickly reached to my right and put my hand over Karen's mouth to prevent her from blurting out rudely, "You are a what?!"

Then, out of natural curiosity, the man asked me the obvious next question, "Oh really, what do you speak about?"

Uh oh, I hadn't gotten that far.

Though I didn't know it yet, the decision had been made. It was only days later that I announced somewhat nervously to my mentor of nine years, "Steve, I'm off to pursue a different path!" It was done. He wished me well.

To be certain, decision and clarity don't always go together. One week after my choice to leave The Fortune Group, I sat down for lunch with a speakers' bureau owner. Speakers' bureaus help corporations and associations find speakers for meetings and conferences.

Over lunch, this seasoned bureau owner asked me a terrific question, "John, if I'm to sell you to my clients, I need to know what you are going to speak about."

I had heard a variation of that question before, hadn't I? This time I was ready with the perfect answer. Like most young, new-to-the-circuit speakers, I responded, "Anything and everything!"

She smiled at my naiveté and calmly rephrased her question, causing me to think more deeply. "John, if we put a gun to your head and during that moment you could only teach one principle, what would it be?"

Never skipping a beat, I smiled and said, "Gun control!"

No, I didn't really say that. What I did say with only a bit of hesitation was "Personal Accountability."

She thought for a moment, then her response came: "You can't do that, it's not a topic."

You know all the topics don't you? Customer service, teamwork, reengineering, management, sales, motivation, time management, diversity, total quality (well, it used to be a topic), and the big one: *change!* She was looking for a box to put me in: a category, a subject, a common phrase, maybe a buzz word or two. A topic the market would buy.

I told her, "But Personal Accountability is what's on my heart. I will talk about it to anybody who will listen!" I'm not certain I saw the market buying it either, but I soon discovered I had hold of a tiger's tail.

Since the day I met with the bureau owner, I've discovered some things. First, the principle of Personal Accountability connects beautifully with just about all the classic *and* popular topics. There is no organization, group or individual the concept cannot help. Not only that, the market *does* want to hear about it. In fact, what's curious is that the market thinks it's "timely." In reality, it's not timely; it's *timeless.* It worked yesterday, it works today and it will work tomorrow. And most importantly, I've come to believe I should not stand before a group and share an idea unless it has made a difference in *my* life. The concept of Personal Accountability more than qualifies, because I can honestly say it *has* changed my life—in many ways.

In fact, the application is so broad, so universal, that, with the help of some very talented people, a learning film was created entitled, *"Personal Accountability and the QBQ."* The film was produced by ChartHouse Learning of Burnsville, Minnesota, the producers of Joel Barker's original film series, "The Business of Paradigms." This film has been acquired by organizations as diverse as Detroit-based automobile makers, a truck stop in the middle of Nebraska and my alma mater, Cornell University. It proves the principle of Personal Accountability is applicable *to everyone, everywhere!*

But the obvious question is: Why did I decide this would be my message? Diane Gulbrandson is one reason.

I called on her early in my sales career when she was vice president of sales for the D.C. Hey Company, at that time a Sharp office products dealer in Minneapolis. She politely listened to the 55-minute one-way monologue I called a sales presentation. I told her about the features, advantages and benefits (known as FABs to salespeople) of the two-day sales management training workshop my company was offering.

Oh, how I wanted her to sign up, along with her four sales managers! I could taste this sale. I poured all my energy into my presentation, taking a big breath at the start and letting it out when I was done, almost an hour later. When I got to the Big Close, she asked to be excused for just a moment. She returned with a piece of paper. This is what it said:

"In one day, David slew a thousand Philistines with the jawbone of an ass. Every day 10,000 sales are killed with the same weapon."

I wonder if she was trying to tell me something.

Diane taught me many things at a time I needed to hear them. It's true: When the student is ready, the teacher appears. And I remember her teaching me this, too: "John, the salesperson is always personally accountable for how the call goes and whether the customer takes action or not."

Diane helped me learn at age 27 that a good salesperson never blames the customer, a principle that has served me well since.

Bob Elgin, St. Jude Medical's vice president of operations, has been another teacher in my life. St. Jude is a manufacturer of heart valves and other medical devices. I have worked with the organization since 1989 and have watched it grow, change and prosper. I've been proud to call the company a client.

About six years into my nine-year career of selling training programs to executives, Bob said something to me I will always remember. It was a passing comment, but it stayed with me. "John, if I were to go out and sell the training you sell, I'd talk to my prospective clients about two things and two things alone: clearly defining expectations, and practicing Personal Accountability. Because those two issues are big problems."

When Bob said that, my mind instantly flashed back to a project I conducted in 1990. I sat in the back of the room serving as the rudder, the guide, the facilitator of a leadership session. This company, a maker of paper products, had just restructured the senior and middle management levels and also had changed the P & L (profit and loss) accounting procedures. There was confusion in the room over who was responsible for what, mixed with anger, frustration and plenty of fear.

This was the executive management team of seven. I can't give you the complete context in which an amazing statement was made, but it has truly been imprinted on my brain forever. The discussion was heating up about strategy and tactics for accomplishing the annual plan just handed down by the company's owners. The newly named president turned to the group and said this about achieving the company's annual profit goal: "Well, I sure don't want that ball!"

This blew my mind. In fact, I thought I'd misheard him, so I leaned over to an associate and he confirmed my ears were working just fine. It seemed the dearth of Personal Accountability was *everywhere*.

I heard the call for Personal Accountability over and over. In 1995, as I was making the transition from selling training to speaking, I invited Ray Barton, president of Great Clips, Inc., to share coffee and wisdom with me. He didn't let me down. He said, "John, if Personal

Accountability is going to be your message, I don't believe you'll have any problem finding work!"

Bill Paxton, a client with Analysts International and a man greatly concerned with principle-based issues, quickly became another friend. The morning after I spoke on the same platform with Lou Holtz to 1,500 people (a dream come true for me, I might add), Bill sent me an e-mail. We had never met. It said, "Since last night I've found the QBQ changing the way I think. This stuff is really powerful." Then for the next year he sent me e-mails, articles and cartoons, all encouraging me to get a book on the market. "Better get your book written on accountability, John," he kept admonishing me. "The world needs it."

A dear friend, Bob Bonkiewicz, called me one Saturday morning after hearing me speak the night before as an after-dinner "keynoter," covering several "Pillar Principles of Prosperity," with Personal Accountability being just *one* of them. He gently instructed me, "John, if you change anything about your presentation, you should give it a heavier emphasis on Personal Accountability. That's what we all need to hear more of every day!"

It took a while, but finally it sank in: I needed to communicate my belief in and passion for Personal Accountability and what this idea can do to transform our organizations and lives. How can I ever repay these people for becoming like a rudder on a ship for me—for candidly telling me what direction to take? I probably cannot, other than to say that without their input and willingness to share from the heart, you would not be holding this book today. And I know that means a great deal to them, as well as to me.

In creating this book, several people became a team of creative consultants. This team has been great fun to work with, especially because they have never lost sight of the objective, not even once, to produce a product that is both powerful and practical, applicable to our professional and private lives.

The team members: David Levin, my speaking coach and friend; Marco Ciavolino, layout and cover designer and man of many ideas; writer Deb Hvass, who captures excellence in all she does, and me. This virtual team is located in Minneapolis, Baltimore, Northfield, Minnesota, and Denver. The four of us spent days and nights communicating via e-mail and phone about every aspect of the book. It makes one wonder how anything ever got accomplished before the Internet.

I'm also grateful to writer Miles Canning for helping me clarify what I wanted to include in the book, and to the professionals at ChartHouse Learning for creating a film the market continues to want and will always need.

Most importantly, I want to thank my wife, Karen, and my four children, Kristin, Tara, Michael and Molly, for their patience in enduring the many rounds of revisions and the erratic work schedule it took to make this book a reality. My deepest gratitude goes to Karen. A man could not ask for a more stalwart supporter, one who at every turn has said, "It's the right message. What can I do to help?"

Thanks, Karen, for being my best friend.

Part 1

The Power of Personal Accountability

Chapter I

The Case for Personal Accountability

"Who's going to solve the problem?"

"Why do we have to go through all this change?"

"When is somebody going to train me?"

"Why doesn't that department do its job?"

"When are my people going to get motivated?"

If you are part of an organization, you probably hear these questions and others like them every day. In fact, you may ask them yourself. I know I do at times. I believe these questions tell us something very important about the person who is asking them—even when I am that person.

I suggest that these questions show a lack of Personal Accountability. Why? Because of their focus. Look at them again. Where is the responsibility being placed? Where are fingers being pointed? Clearly, these questions focus outward, away from the person asking them and toward other people and activities.

When I hear questions such as these, I hear a lack of Personal Accountability. That's because of a key question I do *not* hear: "What can *I* do?"

What is Personal Accountability?

Questions such as "What can I do?" and "How can I make a difference?" demonstrate Personal Accountability. This may seem radical to you, because when you hear the word *accountability,* your first thought may be that of an action or commitment I agree to hold you to or you agree to hold me to.

There certainly can be value in giving and receiving support, but that is not *Personal* Accountability. Personal Accountability is asking, "What can *I* do to make a difference?"

Personal Accountability is *not* a group activity. Accountability groups are popular these days. People get together, make public professions of commitment, then come back a week or a month later to discuss what did or did not happen. This may be a healthy process for many, but it is not what this book is about.

What we will be exploring together is the idea of choosing to practice Personal Accountability by engaging in accountable thinking and action, and that's a decision you and I can only make for ourselves.

I believe this concept is absolutely invaluable—to us, to those around us and to our organizations. In fact, helping people—including myself—practice Personal Accountability is my mission. Here's how that mission began.

My Introduction to Personal Accountability

Oliver Wendell Holmes said, "The mind once stretched by an idea never returns to its original form." I remember vividly a day when I was challenged—permanently—by a mind-stretching idea.

When I was 29 years old, I had been selling and delivering training programs to corporations for about a year. At an annual conference, Steve Brown, the founder and CEO of the organization I represented, was leading the entire sales group through a challenging, all-day instructional session.

During his presentation, Steve would stop about every half-hour and ask, "Who's accountable for your success or failure?" The first time we all just stared at him. Undeterred, he asked again, "Who's accountable for your success or failure?" Finally, some of us volunteered meekly, "Uh, gee, I guess I am."

The third time he asked the question, every hand went up and we all shouted, "I am!" This drill went on throughout the day. It was a powerful exercise. Yet I discovered something: Every person had heard the same question and made the same verbal affirmations, but the message didn't seem to stick for everybody.

Many people left that meeting saying things such as, "Well, there's no marketing, we get too few leads, the brochures are old and our price is too high." Most went away blaming the company for not giving them what they believed they needed to be successful, making excuses for not being able to reach goals and objectives or not intending to do anything to make a difference.

The Blame Game

Once you start listening for it, you'll hear evidence of this kind of thinking everywhere you go. I was in a gas station convenience store looking for some coffee, and discovered the carafe was empty. I said to the guy behind the counter, "Pardon me, there's no coffee in the pot." He half gestured at a co-worker not 15 feet away stocking shelves and muttered, *"Coffee is her department!"* Department? In a roadside gas station the size of your living room?

Not long after that, I was pacing the floor at a pizza place waiting for my carryout order. I was frustrated because they had lost our order. My family was sitting in the car and we were in a hurry. The person behind the counter didn't seem to have much to do, but I sensed he was watching me walk back and forth. Suddenly, out of the blue, he declared, *"Hey, don't blame me, my shift just started!"*

Another example: The plane I was on landed smoothly and rolled to the gate. When the seat belt sign finally went off, 200 passengers jumped to their feet, anxious to get going. But no one was going anywhere. We stood there ... and stood there ... and stood there. Finally, we heard the pilot's deep, confident voice: "Folks, it seems operations is having some problems getting the jet-way up to the plane door. Could you all have a seat while we take care of this small problem? It'll be just a few minutes." Groaning, everybody sat down again. Then the captain returned by intercom to say, "Just so you know, folks, *we in the cockpit have the plane parked right on the money*"!

Now what did that accomplish? His real problem was a planeload of frustrated passengers who probably couldn't care less who was to blame. Did letting us know it wasn't his fault make us any happier with the situation? No. Did it leave us with the impression of his airline that he would have wanted to make? Probably not.

By pointing his finger elsewhere, the captain did nothing to help with the real problem and at a deeper, subtler level may have created more problems. That's the price we pay for a lack of Personal Accountability. At best, nothing gets done and we miss opportunities to make a difference. And often, we actually make things worse.

Avoiding Blame: Silos and Empire Building

I was sitting with Kevin, a vice president of manufacturing, in his spacious, elegant conference room. We were there to discuss some of his critical business issues. Expecting a long dump of woes and concerns, I got out a legal tablet and, my best pen in hand, got ready to take copious notes.

"Tell me, Kevin, what are the concerns you're facing in your business today?"

He said, "John, I can sum it all up in a few words: 'silos and butt covering.'"

Maybe Kevin's choice of words was a little coarse, but I'll bet anyone involved in an organization understands what he meant. I sure did, not only because I had called on organizations for so long, but also because I grew up on a farm. I could see in my mind a tall, windowless, cylinder-shaped structure.

Yes, I've been in a real farm silo. I know what happens in there: Things rot! It's called "silage" and it is bad news. I am acutely aware of how dark and dank it can be in a silo and what the odor is like. I also know how hard it is to see out of one when you're inside. This silo mentality is present every day in organizations, too. While sitting with Kevin, I could visualize people hiding in their silos, usually called departments, isolating themselves to avoid being blamed for errors, disappointing results and other problems.

Do you see that happening in your organization? Do you hear people claiming in some way, "That's not my job," while the divisions and boundaries between departments, groups, locations and people grow taller, stronger and more difficult to overcome? My experience tells me you probably do.

One woman told me that this "silo thing" has been a real problem for her company. "It used to be if someone tried to climb out of their silo to build bridges across department lines, they got pushed back down and told they didn't have enough to do. And sometimes, people who tried to reach across the barriers were labeled 'empire builders'!"

What are the silos in your organization? Are they called accounting, sales, manufacturing, marketing, research & development, operations, administration, the home office, the field? One company's field sales force refers to its own headquarters as the "Sales Prevention Club"! When we see these isolated silos at work, what we're really seeing is a consequence of the lack of accountable thinking and action, the lack of Personal Accountability.

Personal Accountability Cannot Wait

I have come to believe that we often teach others what we ourselves need to hear. What I need to hear and apply each day as a father of four, a best friend to my wife, Karen, an author and a resource to the corporate world is Personal Accountability. And why is that? I need to hear this message because it's so easy to slip from that path. And from my observations, Personal Accountability is also rarely applied in our organizations.

The good news is that organizations can cultivate Personal Accountability. All we have to do is recognize that it starts with our own thinking, and then begin asking different questions such as, "What can I do?" and "How can I contribute?"

I'm absolutely convinced from working with organizations of all types that we can do this. I know what a difference it makes when we think and act accountably. That's what's so exciting. But first, we have to *want* to think and act accountably. If there's a frustration in all this for me, it is the realization that not everybody wants to.

I had been calling on a vice president of a mortgage company to see how this message could be of help to him. After repeated attempts to reach him by phone, I sent him an e-mail message suggesting a presentation to his team. He sent me the following response:

> From: Paul
>
> To: John
>
> Subject: Your request to speak at our company
>
> John, I don't want to continue ignoring you, but the timing is not right. We have several major initiatives we're working on right now.

> The concept of personal accountability, unfortunately,
> is going to have to wait.

I don't believe Personal Accountability can wait. If you agree, read on. In the rest of this book, we'll explore a powerful and practical idea called The Question Behind the Question™ that can help each of us think and act accountably. We'll also see how this idea can make a real difference in our organizations and our lives.

At any given moment, in any situation, in any area of our lives, when we're faced with a decision, I believe Personal Accountability is always the better choice. It's a better way to think, to work and to live. So let's continue on now and explore how The Question Behind the Question can help each of us practice Personal Accountability.

Making Personal Accountability Personal

Take a few minutes to consider the ideas in this first chapter and jot down your thoughts, while they're still fresh in your mind, on a clean sheet of paper.

1. What is one problem I've found frustrating lately at work? At home?

2. What impact has that problem had on my daily effectiveness?

3. Until now, who have I been thinking is responsible for this situation?

4. If I were to practice Personal Accountability regarding this problem, what would I now do differently?

Go ahead and take those actions that come to mind, today.

Chapter II

THE QUESTION BEHIND THE QUESTION

On a hot July day, I was thinking about the organizations I work with when this question came to mind:

"What can I do today to add value to my clients' lives?"

The answer came to me: Karmelkorn! You know—that great-tasting, sticky, caramel-covered popcorn. Normally, I associate it with the big gift-wrapped tins that proliferate around the holidays. So I thought getting one in the middle of summer would be a fun, unexpected treat for my clients. I also thought it would be best to get it there on a Friday since Fridays are usually more casual in companies and often perceived as a "fun" day.

It was already Thursday, though, and I had a full day of sales calls ahead of me. So on my way out the door, I handed someone a piece of paper with my clients' names and addresses on it. "Could you please do me a favor and call the Karmelkorn place and have those big, gift-wrapped tins delivered overnight to the five clients on this list?" I asked.

"Sure," she said, "no problem." Great! I thought.

When I returned later in the day, I checked in with her: "Any problems getting them out?"

"Nope, not a one!" she said cheerfully.

"And it wasn't too late to get them out overnight?" I asked.

Long pause …

"Overnight? You wanted them to go overnight?"

"Yes, I wanted them to be there tomorrow. You know, Friday—corporate casual, fun day. Won't it be great to have my customers eating that corn, reading the card, enjoying the …"

I stopped mid-sentence. "They didn't go overnight, did they?" The response? "How about five-day ground UPS?"

Now, I realize that Karmelkorn not getting shipped overnight is not a serious issue—at least not in this case. But let me ask you a couple of questions:

How do you respond when things don't go as you had planned?

How do you react when things just don't work out the way you hoped they would?

Are you ever disappointed? Do you sometimes get angry? I have those reactions, too. So here's how I was responding and reacting in that moment. In my mind, these thoughts came quickly:

"Weren't you listening?"

"Why didn't you do it the way I asked?"

"Do I have to do put everything in writing?"

And, of course, the big one:
"Must I do everything myself?"

Fortunately, though, the questions got no further, because in spite of the temptation, I stopped short of asking them. Instead, I asked myself a couple of different questions:

"What could I have done to avoid this problem?"

"How could I have communicated more effectively?"

When I asked those questions, everything suddenly looked and felt quite different. So I said, "That's all right. Not a big deal. Thanks for helping me out. I really do appreciate it."

About an hour later, she came to me and said something I'll never forget: "Thanks for not getting upset over the client gifts. I sure wish I had shipped them overnight!"

And as I looked into my *wife Karen's* eyes, I saw and I felt my reward for having made a better choice in that moment.

Karen and I had some good, honest communication that day and it was great. What made the difference were the questions we asked. I asked, "What could I have done to prevent this problem?" instead of, "Why didn't they get shipped correctly?" And Karen asked, "What could I have done to prevent this problem?" as opposed to, "Why didn't you give me better instructions? I've never done this before, you know!" (She hadn't, by the way. She was just helping me out for that one day.)

The Answers Are in the Questions

When we're faced with a challenge or frustration of some kind, our first instincts are usually to protect ourselves and look elsewhere for someone to blame. For most of us, these are automatic defense mechanisms, and they come so naturally that we rarely stop to think about how we are reacting to a given situation.

As a result, the first questions we tend to ask are outwardly focused, as in the story about the Karmelkorn: "Why doesn't *she* … ?" "When will *she* … ?" Those are the easier questions, the ones that come naturally. And they are usually negative questions, which call for negative answers.

Here are some examples:

• When a big sale falls through, we wonder, "When will the customer understand we're the best?"

• When we're passed over for a promotion, we ask, "Why did this happen to me?"

- When people fail to perform their assigned tasks, it's natural to respond with, "When are they going to follow through?"

- When a deadline is missed, the first inclination may be to inquire, "Who blew it?"

Look at those questions again, one by one, and think about the underlying problem in each case. Is any one of those problems going to be improved by getting the answer to its question? I don't think so. That's why it is so important to ask the right questions. The answers are in the questions.

Yet it is so reflexive to ask those outwardly focused questions, the first ones that come to mind. Because of their outward, negative focus, they keep us from discovering and implementing the only real solutions—the ones we have the power to carry out.

I suggest that when we look *behind* those initial questions, we will invariably find better and more challenging questions such as, "What can I do to make a difference?" And these questions will lead us to better answers.

The Question Behind the Question

When I was selling leadership, team-building and sales training systems to corporations, I conducted 10,000 hours of workshops over nine years at all organizational levels. I constantly heard people asking questions that led them nowhere quickly. Maybe you've heard them, too. They were questions such as these: "Who dropped the ball?" "Why don't they help me more?" "When is my manager going to spend more time with me?" Why aren't my people more motivated?"

There were many others like these. I heard a lot of them come out of the mouths of a lot of people—often.

One day I discovered that I, too, had been asking the wrong questions. Then a startling thought occurred to me: If I dig a little deeper and apply some personal discipline, I can ask a better question, which leads to a better answer. I call it The Question Behind the Question (QBQ).

Picture yourself walking into the kitchen for a snack. You open the cupboard door, and the first things to meet your eye are packages of Twinkies and Ho Ho's. You realize they're unhealthy, but they're so close, so tempting, so easy to grab. You know, though, that if you take the effort to push them aside and reach a little deeper—behind the junk—you will find a bag of nonfat pretzels. The pretzels may not be as appealing at the moment, but in the long run they will bring you more rewards than eating junk food. That's the QBQ. It just takes some effort, some discipline, to push aside the junk questions—those that are focused outwardly—and ask The Question Behind the Question.

The Question Behind the Question is more difficult to ask than the initial question, because it's the accountable question, the one that explores what *I* could have done to prevent the problem or what *I* can do in the future. Like seeking out the healthy snack rather than automatically grabbing the junk food, asking the QBQ is a learned response—one that doesn't come naturally.

An effective question (and that's what the QBQ is) such as, "What can I do?" or "How can I contribute?" leads me to doing what is not natural for most of us—living a life of Personal Accountability. For that reason, it usually is not the automatic question that comes to mind in a difficult moment. The QBQ only becomes apparent when I stop and listen to myself and check my reactions to determine what kind of questions I am asking.

That's why it's called The Question *Behind* the Question. If, in the hurry of the moment, we can dig a little deeper and look behind the initial question we're so tempted to ask, we can find a better question.

Let's look once more at the list of questions earlier in this chapter, and for the purpose of this discussion, let's call them Incorrect Questions or IQs.

IQ: When a big sale falls through, we wonder, **"When will the customer understand we're the best?"**

How much better would it be if salespeople everywhere asked, *"How can I better understand the customer?"*

IQ: When we're passed over for a promotion, we ask, **"Why did this happen to me?"**

What if everyone asked, *"What can I do in my current job to excel?"* Wouldn't that make a real difference in your organization and for the individual? You bet it would!

IQ: When people fail to perform their assigned tasks, it's natural to respond with, **"When are they going to follow through?"**

Imagine how much more effective you and I could be if each of us asked: *"How can I contribute today?"*

IQ: When a deadline is missed, the first inclination may be to inquire, **"Who blew it?"**

Here's a better question: *"What can I do to help solve the problem?"*

When we compare IQs with the better questions, it's easy to see what a tremendous difference simply asking better questions can make. And that's what The Question Behind the Question is all about.

The QBQ and Personal Accountability

I am committed to the QBQ because this concept has made a real difference for me. I still feel disappointed when things don't go the way I expect or hope. I still get angry sometimes. But using the QBQ helps me put my initial thoughts on hold, like touching the pause button on a remote control. When my natural inclination in the heat of the moment is to focus on someone or something outside of my control, I can pause my thinking and ask a different kind of question. I can ask the QBQ.

The QBQ is based on the overarching principle that touches all areas of our lives: Personal Accountability. In fact, the QBQ is the "how to" for practicing Personal Accountability. Once you stop and listen to the questions you are asking, you have a choice to make: Identify the QBQ, which leads to Personal Accountability, or ask the questions that come naturally, which accomplishes nothing for our organizations or ourselves. It's your choice—and mine, too.

The QBQ Really Works

Lee Baumann, vice president of agencies for State Farm Insurance, who learned the QBQ at a fall conference, told me months later, "When faced with leadership issues, I consistently use the QBQ to reframe my thinking before I speak or act. It works!"

I honestly believe that most people want to take the high road, the path of Personal Accountability. But I also know that those first, easy questions are very tempting. The bad news is this: Every time we ask them, they take us down the wrong road. The good news is that we can learn to ask better questions. We can learn to think and act accountably, and the QBQ helps us achieve that.

Making the QBQ Personal

In the next chapter, we'll take a closer look at the QBQ. Meanwhile, consider these questions:

1. Can I think of a recent situation in which I automatically asked a negative, outwardly focused question? What answer comes to mind?

2. Take this opportunity to think about and write down a better question—an accountable one such as, "What can I do?" or "How can I contribute?"

3. What answers come to mind for my specific situation?

4. Based on my answers, what actions will I take?

Chapter III

THE QBQ, IN-DEPTH

Here's our working definition of The Question Behind the Question:

*A **method** of **leadership thinking** that enables me to practice **Personal Accountability** by making a better **choice** in the moment*

There it is. I've highlighted the key words. Let's take a look at them one by one.

Method

*A **method** of leadership thinking that enables me to practice Personal Accountability by making a better choice in the moment*

A method is a systematic procedure, way, technique or process for doing something.

Essentially, a method is a "how to." We need a "how to" for Personal Accountability because for most of us, thinking and acting accountably does not come naturally. It must be learned. And since the QBQ is a method, we can learn it.

We'll get into the specific techniques for applying the QBQ in the next few chapters, but for now what's important to know is this: One of the reasons the QBQ is such a great tool is that it is not merely a motivational message. It is truly an effective method. In other words, it's practical. Because the QBQ is a "how to," we can use it to learn how to practice Personal Accountability.

Leadership

*A method of **leadership** thinking that enables me to practice Personal Accountability by making a better choice in the moment*

Are you a leader? Many people who are considered "individual contributors" wrestle with this concept, asking, "Am I a leader or is my boss the leader? Is the company president the leader? The vice president of my division?" Or they think, "Maybe the leader is my peer who was given the title of Team Leader."

The subject of leadership spawns a lot of confusion. I actually heard one front-line associate at a large corporation (a company that was working very hard to create a team culture) say that his personal goal as a leader was to become the *boss* of a self-directed work team!

Seriously though, I believe we are all in leadership roles. A receptionist greeting us in the lobby can be a leader. An engineer designing a new product or application for the customer may be a leader. A salesperson alone in the field a thousand miles from headquarters or the temporary staff person filling in at your company can be leaders. Yet we sometimes lose this perspective.

There probably are as many definitions of leadership as there are leaders. Instead of providing one more, let me share with you what I believe leadership is *not*. You can't predict people's leadership effectiveness by their titles or positions, their tenure with the company, their income or the number of people they manage. The person in the position of manager may or may not be a leader. The vice president may or may not have great leadership skills. And certainly the things we acquire—fine cars, nice homes—are not measures of our leadership ability, either.

Leadership is about something else entirely: It's about the way we think. And true leaders are those whose thinking is characterized by Personal Accountability. Throughout this book, we'll be talking about, studying and celebrating people who are leading in many roles. I hope you will see that we can all be leaders, regardless of our position or situation.

Thinking

*A method of leadership **thinking** that enables me to practice Personal Accountability by making a better choice in the moment*

The QBQ is a thought-shaping tool. We can use it daily to help us practice a better way of thinking. The human mind is the most powerful tool we have, and the better we learn to use it, the more we will accomplish. As Web Edwards says, "The organization that is 'brain rich' will win out over the organization that is cash rich!" Edwards is a leader with Norwest Corporation, a financial services organization.

We are nothing more, nothing less, than products of our thinking. "As I think today, I am tomorrow!" a popular adage claims—and I agree. The exciting thing is that we all can take charge of our own thinking, and learning to control our thoughts may be the most important thing we can do for ourselves and those around us.

It is not always easy, though. Rob Carr, CEO of Redline HealthCare, a distributor of thousands of medical products, once said to me right after a talk I'd given, "I suppose you don't get many standing ovations, do you?" "Why would you say that, Rob?" I asked apprehensively.

His reply was insightful. "Because the QBQ idea makes people think so darn hard. I know it did me!" Accountable people, though, do that—they think darn hard, even when it hurts.

"We cannot solve tomorrow's problems with yesterday's thinking," Einstein once said (paraphrased). We need to change our thinking, and we can do it by asking The Question Behind the Question.

Personal Accountability

A method of leadership thinking that enables me to practice **Personal Accountability** *by making a better choice in the moment*

It was a humid day in Houston. As I boarded the plane, I could feel the heat in the steamy, crowded cabin. The flight had obviously been overbooked, and every passenger seemed to have three pieces of over-sized carry-on luggage. On top of that, there were a few people who apparently had been assigned the same seats, and they weren't taking it very well. Tension in the cabin was high. Finally, the doors closed and we pulled to the runway—only to sit for another hour with no explanation from the crew! I couldn't help but think this gave a whole new meaning to the words "pressurized cabin." We finally took off, and that's when I met Bonita.

Bonita was working as a flight attendant and when I first saw her, she was prancing down the aisle carrying headphones. This was in the coach section, yet she wasn't saying, "We held you up for an hour but give me five bucks anyway!" She was handing the headphones out at no charge. She turned, smiling, to a young man and said, "I'm sure you'll enjoy our sports programming, sir. Here are some headphones." As she handed headphones to a woman, she said, "I notice you're traveling alone, Ma'am, would you like a friend?"

Besides her smile, she was wearing a red-and-white Santa Claus cap, which draped down her shoulder and off to one side. It was about a week before Christmas. When she handed me my headphones, I stopped her and said, "You know, Bonita, I really appreciate your attitude!"

As she pranced away with that big smile on her face and the Santa Claus cap on her head, she said, "Well, whatever you do, don't drug test me!"

Let's face it, nobody needed to test Bonita to know she was "high" on life. And that's one of the great things that happens when we make better choices: We feel better.

Put yourself in Bonita's situation for a moment and consider all the things she could have been thinking:

"Who do these customers think they are, bringing on all this luggage?"

"Why don't they follow the rules?"

"When is someone going to help me out?"

"Why did I get stuck on this crummy flight?"

Or how about,

"Who overbooked the plane?"

"When will those operations people get their act together?"

"Why is this happening to me?"

If I were in Bonita's place, I know I would have been thinking at least some of those questions, if not asking them out loud.

In fact, most of the passengers would have understood if Bonita had asked negative, outwardly focused questions, but where would those questions have taken her? Do you think her customers would have been delighted with her service if she had asked those Incorrect Questions? Probably not. Do you think she would have been enjoying herself as much as she obviously was? Not a chance.

Like Bonita, we should remember to ask ourselves questions such as, "How can I contribute?" "What can I do to make a difference right now?" or "How can I make a positive impact on my frustrated customers?" That's Personal Accountability, and it makes a real difference, for everyone involved, every time.

Choice

*A method of leadership thinking that enables me to practice Personal Accountability by making a better **choice** in the moment.*

A choice is a fork in the road. It's a decision point where we can go right or left, stand still or turn back. When we make a wrong choice, we can get off into the mud, the weeds or the briar patch. I know from experience. Behind our house in Denver we have an acre of prairie, dense with burrs. They're called goat heads because these tiny, prickly thorns have what look like the ears, horns and nose of a goat. After we've been out there, we find them stuck on everything. They're on our socks and pants, and sometimes in our shoes. Let me tell you, when you get a goat head in your shoe, you experience some real pain!

Our choices can cause pain, too, by taking us into life's "Field of Goat Heads." Or they can bring joy, leading us to a richer, more fulfilling life. I know that a lot of people get stuck with the burrs called, "I Have To," "I Can't," "I Must," or "I Must Not," but the fact is that we do have choices, and we make them constantly, every day of our lives. Even deciding not to choose is making a choice.

Not many things are as freeing as when we truly recognize our power to choose. To know we can make better choices in that small, fleeting chance in time we call a moment is very powerful. I admit it can be painful, but mostly it's exciting, and sometimes exhilarating. Benjamin Franklin once said, "Those things in life that hurt, instruct." It's true. We learn with every difficult choice we make, even when it hurts.

This is the essence of the QBQ: We make our own choices, and we're free to make better ones. How many choices do we make all day long? More than we can count. We can decide whether to live on the high road as Bonita demonstrated, or on the low road with a goat head in our shoe. It all comes down to making better choices in the moment.

Now we've come to the end of our QBQ definition, but we're only at the beginning of our QBQ exploration. In the next few chapters, we'll get into the method of the QBQ by exploring the specific disciplines we can use to practice the QBQ and experience the power of Personal Accountability.

Making the QBQ Definition Personal

First, let's look again at the definition of the QBQ.

A method of leadership thinking that enables me to practice Personal Accountability by making a better choice in the moment

Before you start on the next chapter, take a few minutes to think about these two questions:

1. Which key word in the QBQ definition means the most to me and why?

2. Based on the definition alone, how would I change myself and my current approach to both my work and home life?

Now, it's time to execute the actions that come to mind and reap the rewards that will result.

Chapter IV

THE HOW-TO OF THE QBQ: DISCIPLINE ONE

So far, we've discussed some IQs, or Incorrect Questions, and the negative impact they have on our lives. We've also seen how the QBQ can improve our lives. But we haven't talked much about what exactly makes a question a QBQ.

There are three specific disciplines that are essential for creating a QBQ, and in this and the next two chapters, we'll take a look at them one by one. They are *disciplines* because to apply them requires that we exert conscious effort and energy. But once learned, they are invaluable. As with all disciplines, the QBQ disciplines become habits only through repeated application.

Discipline One: All QBQs begin with "What" or "How," not "Why," "When" or "Who."

Avoid questions beginning with "Why."

When we begin a question with "Why," in essence what we're saying is "Poor me!" Look at the questions below. Run them through your mind. Roll them aloud off your tongue.

"Why is this happening to me?"

"Why did they do that to me?"

"Why do we have to go through all this change?"

"Why doesn't the customer call me back?"

"Why do they make it so difficult for me to do my job?"

How do you feel when you say and hear them? They make me feel powerless—like a victim. When we ask questions that have a "Why me?" tone to them, what we're really saying is, "I'm a victim of the environment and the people around me." Not a very productive thought, is it?

Unfortunately, we can observe the symptoms of Victim Thinking all around us. Most people don't consciously tell themselves, "I want to think like a victim," but when Victim Thinking works its way into our minds, it becomes evident in the questions we ask.

Victim Thinking: The Thief in the Night

Where does Victim Thinking come from? I believe it sneaks up on us like a thief in the night. There was a jeweler in the southeastern United States who went out of business in the early '90s because of a thief. The thief was a man with a vendetta against the store owner, yet the thief never removed a watch, a broach, a ring or a pendant. This may sound impossible, but believe me, it is a true story. How did the jeweler go out of business? He was not vigilant. Here's what the thief did: Each week over a series of months, he stole silently into the shop and reduced prices on every item by a few percentage points. The jeweler unwittingly broke the Number One Rule of Business: *Never run out of cash.*

Victim Thinking is like the thief. It exists for one purpose: to defeat us. It steals silently into our thoughts, influences our emotions and changes our behaviors. It is a human tendency and can only be overcome if we exercise our leadership skills to control our thoughts.

I spoke one evening in Charlotte, North Carolina, and the next day received an e-mail message from a member of the audience. He told me that during his 10 years in the military, when something went wrong, the only acceptable response was, "I dropped the ball, no excuses!" He accepted it, he believed it and he lived it. "No excuses."

When he returned to civilian life, he started working as a salesperson in the corporate world. He wasn't doing as well as his company expected, and *he* wasn't pleased with his performance, either. The morning before the program on Personal Accountability, in fact, he had gone to his sales manager and asked questions such as these:

"Why don't you give me more of your time?"

"Why don't you coach me more?"

"Why don't we get some new products?"

"Why are our prices so high?"

"Why don't I get more of your support?"

He closed his message to me saying, "I realized when I learned about the QBQ that from military to business, in just a few short years, I had become what I hated the most: the victim!"

If this man, after 10 years of living and breathing "no excuses" can slip into Victim Thinking, it's no wonder the rest of us have to be on the lookout for it in our own lives.

Another conversation I had recently with a man also was intriguing. He and I sat next to each other on a cross-country flight. Before I tell you what he does for a living, let me mention what he owns. He has a second home near Aspen and when I talked with him, he had just completed a 21-day ski vacation. That's right, twenty-one days! Do you think this man has some discretionary income? If you're curious about what he does, he's a personal injury attorney who lives in New York City and offices on Wall Street.

At one point in the conversation he asked me, "John, what do you do for a living?"

At times like this, I tend to opt for the quick, easy answer, so I said, "I'm a speaker."

"Oh really, what do you speak about?"

I considered his question for a moment and thought, Why not? So I looked him in the eye and said, "Personal Accountability."

I let another moment pass before I stated bluntly, "What I really do is help people eliminate *Victim Thinking* from their lives." After that, he turned toward the window and we didn't talk for two hours!

It's nothing against him and his profession. He's simply supplying what is demanded by a society that continually asks, "Why is this happening to me?" But think about it: The demand for his services would all but disappear if each of us eliminated Victim Thinking from our lives. Instead of asking, "Why did that person give me whiplash?" we could be asking, "What could I have done to prevent the accident?" And, if we're honest with ourselves, often there are many things we could have done.

Getting Rid of Victim Thinking

Of course, there really are things in our lives beyond our control: random events, people we depend on who don't follow through, market competition and a fast-changing environment. So I'm not blaming anyone for falling into the Victim Thinking trap. What I am saying is that we are all better off when we spend as little time as possible thinking like victims.

Personally, I can't think of one benefit of Victim Thinking. So let's avoid questions beginning with "Why."

Now an "Exorcising Exercise." It helps when we acknowledge unhealthy patterns in our lives so we can work to eliminate them. On a sheet of paper, list a few "Why" questions you've been asking.

After you've written them down, take your pen or pencil and cross them out. Congratulations! You just took the first step toward eliminating Victim Thinking from your life. Doesn't that feel great? From now on, you can use the QBQ to do the same thing.

Avoid questions beginning with "When."

I decided to give away a very large, old wooden desk, topped with a piece of quarter-inch-thick clear glass, about three feet by five feet. The new owner didn't want the glass. When we loaded the desk into his truck early one Saturday morning, we left the sheet of glass leaning against a basketball hoop pole at the edge of our driveway.

As my friend drove away with the desk, he said, "You'd better put that glass in a safe place." I yelled back, "I will!" But I didn't. I glanced at it and told myself I'd do it later. Then I got busy working around the lawn, trimming bushes and cleaning the garage. Every time I walked by that sheet of glass I told myself that I should move it before it blew over. I'll do it later, I kept thinking.

The day wore on and my family of six decided to go out for dinner. As we backed out of the driveway, my wife, Karen, said, "Shouldn't we put that glass someplace safe?" You know what I told her.

A couple of hours later, we arrived home in the dark and were all heading into the house when I spotted some small grass clippers sitting near the curb under a street light. I said to our son, Michael, who was nine, "Mike, would you go over there and grab those clippers and put them in the garage for me, please?" Off he went as I headed into the house.

It was a quiet Saturday evening in our pleasant neighborhood, until the silence was broken by the most terrifying sound I have ever heard: the shattering of glass.

I realized immediately what had happened. I also knew why. I dashed out of the garage and around our car to find Mike lying in the driveway on his stomach atop hundreds of deadly shards of glass, some more than a foot long. He was crying as I ran, carrying him, to the front porch. I held him under the light to check his injuries, expecting the worst, and I couldn't believe what I saw: not a scratch! He had run right into the glass and fallen on top of it as it hit the pavement, but there wasn't a mark on him. To say we felt incredibly thankful would be an understatement.

Why did this incident happen? Procrastination, the Friend of Failure. We were fortunate in that, at least this time, my negligence did not carry a high cost. But the cost of procrastinating is often very high. Time is lost, energy is wasted, issues don't get addressed and problems linger, usually getting worse over time.

Why do we procrastinate? We could dig deep into the psychological reasons, but frankly, I'd rather not. I'd prefer to talk about a solution instead. And one solution is to stop asking externally focused questions that begin with "When":

"When will they take care of the problem?"

"When will the customer get back to me?"

"When will the people in that department do their jobs?"

"When will the CEO share the vision?"

"When will someone clarify my job?"

"When will my teammates do what they're supposed to do?"

Questions that begin with "When" lead us straight to Procrastination. I don't think we intend to procrastinate. Would you go into a meeting tomorrow, raise your hand and say, "Hi, I am a procrastinator!"? No. (You'd probably put it off until the next meeting, right?) But as with Victim Thinking, Procrastination sneaks up on us. We find ourselves putting things off longer and longer until our lack of action becomes a problem.

When Things Are Beyond Our Control

You may be thinking, "But there are times when things really are beyond my control. How can the QBQ help me when I get stuck waiting on someone else to take action?"

I was presenting at a major insurance company and a sales agent approached me during a break. "John, I have a problem," she said. "I have a customer with a unique health history and I've been trying to get her application for insurance approved. But I've called my regional office a half dozen times and *my own company* won't call me back! My customer needs an answer and I can't seem to get her one."

I felt bad for her. She naturally felt bad for herself, as well as for her customer. Who would hold it against her? I saw in her eyes the frustration and anguish of trying to do a good job and not being able to get it done. The temptation must have been very strong to ask questions such as these: "When are they going to get back to me?" "When will the people in underwriting do their jobs?" and "When is someone going to take care of this?"

When she asked me what to do, I reminded her that the answers are in the questions. We reviewed the QBQ disciplines and she returned to her seat with a new frame of mind. Why? Because she chose to ask a better question: "What *else* can I do to solve this problem?"

Later, she said she just might drive down to the regional office, march into the regional vice president's office without an appointment and confront the issue head on. Risky? Perhaps. But the path she had been taking was paved only with frustration and stress, leading to costly inaction. She could have continued in that direction and fallen prey to Procrastination, but she had already seen (from her company's example) what that accomplished. Not much.

Don't Just Sit There

When we sit back and wait rather than take action, we are not practicing Personal Accountability. Personally, I'd rather charge ahead and be told to wait, than wait to be told what to do. Sure, this means taking more risks, but overcoming Procrastination often means overcoming inertia in order to accomplish a challenging task—and that requires risk.

A senior leader of a financial institution told me, "Sometimes people say to me, 'I don't want to take risks.' I tell them, 'You and I had better take risks, because there are about a dozen people at their computers right now in the back room of this organization trying to *eliminate* our jobs!'" What was he really saying? Each of us needs to add value and we only add value when we *do* something, not when we ask questions beginning with, "When will they ... ?" or "When is he going to ... ?"

It's so simple, yet so effective. When we choose to think accountably, we act. When we act, we add value to our organization, to those around us and to our own lives.

Now, let's exorcise the Friend of Failure from our lives by writing down any IQs we have been asking that begin with "When," and then crossing them out.

Avoid questions beginning with "Who."

"Who made the mistake?"

"Who dropped the ball?"

"Who missed the deadline?"

When we ask questions such as these, what we're really doing is looking for scapegoats; we're looking for someone to blame. This type of IQ, one that starts with "Who," may be my favorite one to eliminate because Blame is the absolute opposite of Personal Accountability.

Blame: The Company Coat of Arms

Often in presentations, I will demonstrate a physical posture I call "The Company Coat of Arms," by folding my arms across my chest and pointing all my fingers at everyone except myself. This image symbolizes the mind-set we possess when we ask Incorrect Questions beginning with "Who": finger-pointing and Blame.

This uniform, worn so often by so many, and the thinking it represents, may well be the most counter-productive of all the ideas we've talked about. Unfortunately, you can see Blame everywhere you turn.

After I had spoken on this subject, a man approached me to tell me his organization believes so strongly in playing the Blame Game, they even put it in their computer system. "Huh?" I asked intelligently.

"Whenever anyone in our company logs on to a certain program, they have to enter their initials on a screen called the 'Blame Field.' That way, if someone messes it up, they know who did it." Amazing.

I was riding in a van from Snowbird Lodge outside Salt Lake City down to the airport. It turned out that the driver doubled as a sales manager for a transportation firm. As we talked about the subject of Blame, he said, "Oh, we've got lots of Blame going on in our company!"

"Really?" I responded, hoping he'd go on.

The man was not shy. "Yeah, the receptionist blames the dispatchers who blame the drivers who blame the salespeople who blame me ... ."

I interrupted him. "How many people are in your firm?"

"Twelve," he said. Twelve people! I guess you don't have to be big to play the Blame Game.

The Circle of Blame

I believe we have an epidemic of Blame in our society. From the smallest group to the largest corporation, no one is immune to Blame. It sneaks into every aspect of our lives. The CEO blames the vice president, who blames the manager, who blames the employee, who blames the customer, who blames the government, who blames the people, who blame the politicians, who blame the schools, who blame the parents, who blame the teen, who blames the mom, who blames the dad, who looks at the wife and says, "Why didn't you ship the Karmelkorn overnight?" (To this day, I'm glad I didn't ask that question of Karen.)

I call that "The Circle of Blame," and it would be kind of funny if it weren't such a big problem, everywhere.

Have you ever participated in a *blamestorming* session? Blamestorming occurs when people get together and generate creative ideas about whom to blame for various problems and perceived failures. When we engage in blamestorming, we're spinning our wheels by asking "whodunit" questions. We not only abandon constructive dialogue, which might solve a problem, but we denigrate other people or departments—or our organization as a whole.

We/They: A Symptom of Blame

Accountable thinking leads to questions such as, "What can I do?" These questions help us make a positive difference. An easy tip-off that someone is asking a Blame-oriented question is the word "they."

Does your organization have a "we/they" syndrome? I had called on corporations for about five years when I realized that *every* company, group or association has one to some extent. That is, until I met one vice president who proudly proclaimed there was no we/they problem in his organization. I exclaimed, "You're kidding! No we/they? No cross-functional friction? No field-versus-corporate mentality? No management-versus-employees attitude? No we/they?" He looked at me with a smirk and said, "Nope, there's no we/they here—but it is *"us"* against *"them"*!

The Blame Game is not always open and obvious. When people in one department of an organization complain they can't do their work because another department is lagging in its performance, it may not sound like Blame, but the effects are the same as if they had pointed a finger and openly said, "It's that department's fault over there." Such statements are clearly founded in the lack of Personal Accountability.

Two Who Didn't Play the Blame Game

Now, I acknowledge that not everybody blames, points fingers and chooses sides. Some people seem to have a natural instinct for accountable thinking.

I was having a problem at the office with static in my phone line, and two different repair people had not been able to fix it. When the third person came, I described the problem, paused and waited for the Blame to roll. I fully expected him to bad-mouth the other two from his own organization, but he didn't. Instead, he said something very powerful: "Mr. Miller, I can't explain this, but I sure can *apologize* for it!" What a breath of fresh air!

Stan Donnelly is another one. He's the CEO of Donnelly Custom Manufacturing Company of Alexandria, Minnesota. The company molds plastic parts for all kinds of products. Donnelly had created the latches and clips for the prototype of some new in-line skates produced by another organization. Unfortunately, someone at Donnelly had put the latches on backward—a simple error that had gotten by unnoticed. Meanwhile, the skate manufacturer's president and a small team took a couple of pairs of skates to Europe to call on a potential distributor. It was there that they opened the box for the first time and found that the latches did not work.

When word got back to the Donnelly organization and the employees talked about what had happened, one person said, "Why didn't they look at the skates and check them out before they left on the trip?"

"No," Stan said forcefully, "that was *our* job!"

Isn't that great? *That's* accountable thinking.

Not everyone plays the Blame Game, but in my experience, far too many of us do, and I include myself in that. I will say, though, that it happens less frequently in my life since I started using the QBQ.

The Cost of Blame

How much does blaming behavior cost us? Everything! The only real resource any company has is its people. No problem gets solved, no challenge gets tackled and no objective gets met until people apply their talents and energy. Finger-pointing and Blame are the ultimate waste of resources because they take a lot of time and energy, and they accomplish nothing.

Imagine what we could do in our organizations, in our families, in our communities and in our lives if we could just eliminate Blame. When fingers point at everybody else, sales, service and productivity usually head south. A company's doldrums usually are not due to market factors, poor sales tactics, old technology or insufficient advertising. They're because of the way people think, because of the way they view each other and themselves. Organizations cannot solve problems, live their missions and achieve their visions when their people choose to blame each other and avoid practicing Personal Accountability.

Fortunately, there is something we can do about these problems, and that something is (how did you guess?) the QBQ!

Are you asking IQ's that begin with "Who"? Are you asking questions that lead to searching for scapegoats and finding fault? If so, jot them down. Now go ahead and cross them out. From this moment, start using the QBQ to erase that kind of thinking from your life.

Making Discipline One Personal

In the next chapter we'll look at Discipline Two: All QBQs contain the word "I." But first, let's review Discipline One: All QBQs begin with "What" or "How," not "Why," "When" or "Who." There's a truth that goes something like this: "Understand yourself, and you understand the entire human race." Part of the process of understanding myself is challenging myself each day to recognize and avoid Victim Thinking, Procrastination and Blame, both in my professional life and in my personal life. I am not a finished product, but by practicing this first discipline of the QBQ, I am improving.

Now, ask—and answer—these questions:

1. Which of these three traps do I slip into most easily?

2. What are the consequences?

3. How can I avoid these unhealthy patterns and improve my life?

4. What specific action(s) will I take today?

Chapter V

The How-to of the QBQ: Discipline Two

In 1991, my wife, Karen, came to me after 11 years of marriage and posed a riveting question. Actually, it felt more like a statement: "Johnny, I'm going to marital counseling. Are you coming?" It knocked the wind right out of me but I said yes, I would go, because in my heart I knew she was right; we needed some help. Forgive me for starting with such a personal story, but the lesson I learned is the foundation of our second QBQ discipline. And this lesson applies not only to marriage, but to all relationships.

Three days later, Karen and I were sitting in the office of our counselor, Terry. He listened patiently as each of us shared about the maddening things the other did. After a half-hour of this, he wisely told us that a lot of our frustration as a couple was coming from our trying to change each other. It didn't take him long to point out how unproductive it was for me to try to change Karen and for Karen to try to change me. It all sounded good to me. "Sure. I see that," I said. "OK, I get it. I need to stop trying to change Karen because I can only change myself."

At our next session a month later, Terry sensed that I was obviously still feeling some frustration. "What's going on with you, John?" he asked.

"Well," I said, "I've been doing everything I can think of to stop trying to change Karen and accept her for who she is, and it's been all this time, and, and ... she still hasn't changed!"

Oops. Did I just say what I think I said? Was I really trying to change her? That was a real eye-opener for me. It was then I began to realize that I was not the *only* person who did this all the time without even knowing it.

The questions we ask often betray our real motives, if we only listen carefully:

"When will my people do their jobs?"

"Why doesn't my boss appreciate all I do?"

"When will the field communicate better?"

"Who in this organization is going to start caring as much as I do?"

"Why doesn't my manager clarify my job?"

This brings us to the second discipline for creating and applying The Question Behind the Question. This discipline is possibly the most challenging, but it just may be the most rewarding:

Discipline Two: All QBQs contain an "I."

Notice I did not say that all QBQs contain a "they," "them," "us," "you" or "we." One of the most tempting things to do with the QBQ once we've decided to embrace it is to ask, "What can *we* do?" The problem is that "we" don't change. In fact, organizations, departments and teams don't change, either. We all know (intellectually, at least) that only individuals can change, one at a time, through their own choices. If I asked you, "Who's the only person you can change?" I'm sure you would have the right answer: "me."

Sometimes, though, we try to change others without realizing it. While the language we use to express our intentions may *sound* helpful and altruistic, on closer examination, our true motives are to change others, not ourselves. We may call it something else or justify it in one way or another, but with all of these questions, the bottom line is the same: We're trying to change someone else.

Subtle Motives

I was working with 12 CEOs from different companies in a half-day workshop. One of the participants, who owned 47 Burger Kings, announced, "I'm going to take my 22-year-old son around the world in two weeks. He just graduated from Yale!" I thought to myself, How terrific to share time together, celebrating the son's graduation from college, just father and son. But my thoughts were jarred back to reality when he added, "Yes, I'm taking him around the world so I can talk him into *joining the family business.*"

Another example: Good salespeople often get promoted to sales management positions. Then they go out on a coaching call and tell the rep, "It's your call today. Handle it any way you want. I'm just here to observe and to help you polish up your presentation." But when the call isn't going well in the manager's opinion, he or she steps in, rescues the salesperson and makes the sale. On the way back to the office, the manager says, "I did that to help you improve your selling skills." Translation: "Sell the way I sell. Be like me."

At a leadership development session I was facilitating for a nonprofit organization, I happened to be walking by a round table discussion when the director was speaking persuasively to four team members. "Really," he implored, "I'm not trying to change my wife. I'm not!" Then he added, "I just want her to set more long-term goals ... like I do." It was code talk for "I want *her* to be what *I* want her to be."

In all of these examples, the outward intention seemed praiseworthy: taking the son around the world, teaching the sales rep or helping someone set long-term goals. But the real objective was to change another person. In our relationship, Karen and I found the same principle at work on a more subtle level.

One evening, we had a heated "discussion," and I concluded that she wasn't abiding by the teachings we had learned in counseling. "You can't change me, so stop trying," I told her.

The next day, we visited Terry, our counselor. I was sure that when we explained what had transpired the night before, he would come to my aid, telling Karen how wrong she was and how she needed to work on changing herself, not me. To my utter disbelief, here's what he said to me:

"John, are you aware that when you defend yourself and try to stop Karen from changing you, you are actually *trying to change her?*"

I was stunned by his statement—and by my realization that it was true. I had directed all of my energy, my wits and creativity at trying to change *her* opinions, *her* feelings and *her* behavior. I was trying to change her and it wasn't working.

Inside our organizations, I've discovered that attempts to change others often are not so subtle.

What Would You Change?

I have a little exercise for you now. If you would, take just a moment and write down an answer to this question:

What one thing would you change to improve the effectiveness of your organization? Take a moment now and jot it down on a piece of paper.

I regularly ask this question of groups. Recently, the day before I was to give a QBQ presentation, an audience was asked for responses to this question, and I read them the night before. For the most part, the answers covered the typical "Ps": Products, Promotions, Policies, Processes, Pricing and People. They wanted more people, fewer people, different people. One respondent wanted Pepsi. Yes, Pepsi. "If only we would switch the pop machine from Coke to Pepsi!" they wrote in earnest as if the bottom line of the organization depended on it. These were the things they would change to improve the effectiveness of their organization. Does your answer fall into one of those categories?

Finally, I saw a written response that wasn't so common. In fact, I had never seen it before, nor have I seen it since. At first I didn't trust my eyes. I strained as I sat at my hotel desk, tilting the paper toward the light. Was it possible? YES! Someone had written, "I would change *me.*" I hope that's what you wrote too.

You may consider this a trick question, but it shows that we need to recognize the difference between *saying* we understand the idea, "Yes, I can only change myself!" and the reality of our thoughts and actions.

Fixing Ed

I was addressing about 500 executives in an evening session when a participant approached me during a break. "John," he said, "I'm not very pleased with the program. I'm not getting what I wanted tonight."

I apologized for his perception that I had let him down, and asked him a few questions. It turned out that he owned a company of 100 employees. When I asked about his expectations for that night's program, his response was, "Well, I knew the session tonight was going to be on Personal Accountability but what I really wanted was some content that would help me *hold all my people accountable.*"

This is classic management thinking: "It's my job to hold everybody else accountable," instead of simply asking, "What can I do differently?" "How can I be more effective?" "What can I do to practice Personal Accountability?"

Then there was the sales manager who wanted to purchase a selling skills training program. The human resources person knew the real reason the manager wanted to buy the training. I was floored when she said it, and she was slightly embarrassed. *"He wants it to 'fix Ed,'"* she said. Ed was a salesperson who was struggling in his job. I've never forgotten those two simple words: "Fix Ed." Poor Ed.

Here's an illustration that is sure to make us think: The CEO of a 1,000-person corporation climbed to the stage after I'd spoken for an hour on Personal Accountability and how I can only change myself.

He came up to close the meeting and to display a slide on the ballroom wall. Sounds innocent enough, but this is what the floor-to-ceiling-high slide said:

"*Personal* Accountability Begins With YOU!"

Please read that a couple of times and let it sink in. Personal Accountability does not begin with them out there. It doesn't even begin with you. It begins with me, because I can only change myself. And this was from the CEO, the leader of the leaders! That brings me to my next point, which is especially for managers.

Managers Are Not Exempt

Do you know who seems to have the hardest time with the concept that we can only change ourselves? Managers. Those with people "under" them—senior vice presidents, supervisors, team leaders, directors, CEOs—often believe this principle does not apply to them.

I say this because every time I'm in front of a group of managers, I get the same message loud and clear, whether through their eyes, their body language or their words: "But John, you don't get it. I'm in charge here. In fact, I've been granted the power to change all the people around me. It's in my job description: I am a *manager!*"

The role of the manager/leader is, among other things, to coach, counsel, share ideas, facilitate, clarify expectations, confront unacceptable behavior and terminate (after documentation, of course). But we *never* change another person. That is a decision made and accomplished from the inside out by the individual, for the individual.

Now, I don't mean to pick on managers, but we all have one attitude or another that can benefit from a fresh perspective and a QBQ or two. I've seen how powerful this whole concept of only changing ourselves can be for managers. Asking "How can I be a more effective coach for you?" and "What can I do to adapt my style to yours?" certainly would be a lot better than pointing the finger through questions such as, "Why aren't you motivated?" or "When will you change?"

Our intentions may be good, and we really may be right that change is needed, but that's not the point. The point is, we can't change others, and the more we try, the more frustrated we will get and the more our relationships will suffer.

Steve, a client of mine, recently retired as the vice president of manufacturing for a large company. In my work with him and his team, I had seen the respect everyone had for him. People said Steve was quite a leader. He had started in a line position with his company and eventually had become a manager.

Steve had always wanted to be a manager. Before long, however, his enthusiasm wore off because he realized that managing people was more difficult than he thought it would be. In fact, he really didn't like his new position. A year later, he was still struggling with it and when he went home for a family reunion, he took his frustration with him.

Over the course of the weekend, his family listened to him endlessly mull over questions such as these: "When are my people going to do their jobs?" "Why don't they do things right?" "When are they going to care as much as I do?"

On his last night at home, he was having coffee with his parents. Before his mother retired for the night, she gently but purposefully pressed an old-fashioned skeleton key into his hand.

"Steve," she said softly, "I want you to keep this key with you for the next month. Every time you reach into your pocket, remember this: You are the key. Steve, *you* are the key!"

That is the message of QBQ Discipline Two. You cannot change others. You can only change yourself. You are the key. When we truly understand and begin to act upon this concept, it changes us from the inside out.

Breakthrough Experiences

There is hope for those who keep trying to do the impossible—change others—and that's most of us. After a presentation, a middle manager told me the QBQ content had really touched her. Here is her story.

"When I was a branch manager, there was a guy reporting to me who I just couldn't seem to manage. We didn't work well together at all. When he transferred to another location across the country, I was glad.

"A couple of years passed and we found ourselves in the same office again. I was his supervisor!

"But this time it was different," she said. "We were getting along, communicating well and cooperating on projects."

It was obvious to me that this experience was a positive one for her. She continued, "At one point I asked myself, 'When did Rob change?' Then, I realized: He didn't change, I did!"

"How did you change?" I inquired.

Her response nailed it right on the head: "I stopped trying to change him!"

Wasn't that a win-win for everyone? I believe it was. And it came from accountable thinking expressed as, "What can I do to change myself?" and "How can I be a more effective leader for you?"

Here's another story that shows the dynamics often involved in learning this concept. I facilitated a session with a half dozen sales managers at a manufacturing company, and from the beginning I could sense the frustration among them. I didn't know then what it was about, but I thought it must have been going on for a while, judging from the level of anger in the room.

As we spent the day together, I began to picture them as a balloon that was too full of air. I was trying to keep it from bursting by stretching the opening between my fingers and slowly letting off the extra pressure. But in place of the high-pitched squeal you get when you do that with a balloon, all day long I heard IQs that began with, "Why don't they … " "When will that department … " and "Who is making the mistakes in … ."

Most of these questions, and the anger behind them, were directed at the organization's internal customer service and operations group, whose job it was to execute the contracts these sales managers and their people brought in from the field. The field group's income was directly affected by the performance of the corporate operations group. So they were venting. Slowly.

Late in the day, with most of the emotional tension and pressure relieved, one regional manager finally sat back, paused and asked this QBQ: "What can *I* do to help them at headquarters?"

It was a breakthrough! Do you hear and feel the difference in the focus, tone and intent? And it was a perfect QBQ: It began with "What," contained an "I" and … . Well, I guess you'll have to wait until the next chapter for the rest.

It's exciting for me to see a breakthrough like this because I know what a difference it will make for them. On one hand, they'll feel less frustration and stress because they're no longer trying to change others. On the other hand, since they're in a more open and cooperative state of mind, they're much more likely to get the support they want from the other group. They will accomplish all this by practicing Personal Accountability, that is, by asking better questions and making better choices.

Such breakthroughs do not always come easily. In fact, realizing that we cannot change others is a lifelong process. It is a lesson I'm continuing to learn each day.

The Day I Finally "Got It"

I remember vividly that day with Karen in Terry's office when I truly realized, on a deeper level, that I could not change her. As I processed what had just happened in my "Aha!" moment, I physically began to feel changes. It was as if a veil had been lifted from in front of my eyes. I smiled and suddenly felt energized and relaxed at the same time, as if I had taken a deep, healthy breath of fresh air.

This was a critical moment for me and it's also a powerful illustration of the underlying benefits of accountable thinking. IQs, beyond leading us to Victim Thinking, Procrastination and Blame, cause frustration. This is because we're trying to do the impossible, control the uncontrollable, change the unchangeable. Frustration is a major stressor. It eats away at our ability to be productive, relate effectively to those around us and enjoy our lives. By asking questions that start with "What" or "How" and contain an "I," we reduce stress and frustration. These questions take the focus off of people and events we can't change or control and put it back on ourselves.

The bottom line is that the QBQ works because it is based on the truth that I can only change myself, and Discipline Two makes that happen: All QBQs contain an "I." It's the "I" that makes a question accountable. And the QBQ is the tool we all can use to put the concept of Personal Accountability into daily practice. How much better do you think things would be if we all tried to mold and shape our own thoughts, feelings and actions rather than those of others? I believe we would be much better off. In fact, Karen and I are living proof. Although our relationship is not perfect, we have experienced far more joy and less stress since we both realized that it is impossible to change each other and instead started focusing on changing ourselves.

Are you familiar with the Serenity Prayer?

"God, grant me the serenity
to accept the things I cannot change,
the courage to change the things I can
and the wisdom to know the difference."

Here's a variation for you:

"God, grant me the serenity
to accept the people I cannot change,
the courage to change the *one* I can
and the wisdom to know ... *it's me!*"

Making Discipline Two Personal

We now have two disciplines: All QBQs begin with "What" or "How," and contain an "I." In the next chapter, we'll learn the third and final QBQ discipline: All QBQs focus on action.

But first, take your pen in hand and commit to an action regarding Discipline Two: All QBQs contain an "I."

Ask yourself these questions:

1. Who have I been trying to change other than myself? If I have not been trying overtly to change the person, how was I doing it in subtle ways?

2. What impact has my attempt to change that person had on the relationship?

3. Since it's true that I can only change myself, what will I now do differently?

Chapter VI

THE HOW-TO OF THE QBQ: DISCIPLINE THREE

In business, buzz words and popular phrases tend to come and go, then come again. In the late '80s, when "strategic planning" was a hot phrase, I visited with a client who said, "You know, John, these three-to-five-year plans are a nice idea, but what I really want to know is what we are going to do today before lunch."

I'm a believer in goals and planning, but I liked what she said. I've never met an achiever who didn't possess a "fire in the belly" to get things done ... now!

Our third discipline, then, for creating a QBQ is this:

Discipline Three: All QBQs focus on action.

To focus QBQs on action, all we need to do is add verbs such as "do," "make," "achieve" and "build" to our questions that start with "What" or "How" and contain an "I."

Now if that's all we did, a QBQ might sound something like, "What I do?" or "How I build?" So to avoid sounding like cave people, we add another word or two such as "can" or "will" and "now" or "today," and end up with excellent-sounding QBQs such as these: "What can I do right now?" and "How will I make a difference today?"

"The answers are in the questions" is a premise we will use throughout the book. If we don't ask, "What can I *do, make, achieve or build?*" then we won't do, make, achieve or build. It's just that simple. It is only through action that we *do* (accomplish) the objective, *make* the sale, *achieve* the goal and *build* the relationship. It is only through our actions that we bring value to our customers and contribute to the lives of others.

Winning through Failure

A client once said to me, "We need people who are sometimes wrong, but never in doubt!" I like that philosophy.

At times we may stumble. At times we'll say and do the wrong thing at the wrong time. Sometimes we will flat-out fail. But good things rarely come from inaction.

For example, successful salespeople often are awarded plaques, trophies and applause at national sales meetings. What is not noted, however, are the stories of failed presentations and annoyed prospects that even successful salespeople collect in the course of doing business. The most successful are those who are able to overcome the fear of failure and rejection that often keeps salespeople from calling on key decision makers so they can make the sale. Although it hurts to fail, I'd rather win through failure. What does that mean? I only learn, change and grow when I act, even if things don't turn out as I expected.

It was once said, "Winners keep falling forward." In other words, they don't win on every attempt, but they do take that next step.

Steve Brown of The Fortune Group, who taught me the "I am!" response to the question, "Who is responsible for your success or failure?" also taught me this: Anything worth doing is worth doing miserably, at least for a while! There are not many things in life we do very well the first time out. Only through repeated action do we improve.

Personal Accountability, The Question Behind the Question, and accountable thinking in general, all ultimately come down to taking action.

The Price of Inaction

Many people have helped me see the value in taking action. Bob Elgin is vice president of operations for St. Jude Medical, a medical device manufacturer. One day I asked him this question: "Bob, have you ever let anyone go because they took an honest action and the result turned out negative?"

"No," he said without hesitation. Then a moment later he added this: "But you know what, John? Come to think of it, I've seen a lot of people leave organizations because they did *nothing!*"

After a corporate engagement at a company where a major merger had occurred, a man told me he had come into the session "complaining, whining and griping" (his words) about a problem at the New Jersey headquarters that affected his field operation. As a result of discovering the QBQ that day, he had slipped out halfway through the session, called his travel agent and booked a ticket for the next day back to the East Coast to help solve the problem.

Had he been paying a price for his prior inaction? Definitely. The stress and frustration underneath his complaining, whining and griping were undoubtedly hurting his general effectiveness and productivity. There will be value in getting the issue confronted and resolved—both for him and for his organization. And what made the difference for him? He told me the QBQ that triggered his decision to act was, "What action can I take right now to solve the problem?" Yes, the answers truly are in the questions.

The Rewards of Taking Action

A district sales manager for American Express Financial Advisors called from Dallas inviting me to present the QBQ to his organization. He then asked me to ship my speaker's press kit (audiotapes, a preview video, folder and reference letters) to him so that his speaker selection committee could review it. I made sure the press kit arrived at his office the next day, Tuesday.

On Friday he called me to confirm the engagement. (Sometimes it takes weeks or months for a confirmation, particularly when a committee is involved.) I asked him what he had done with all my materials, and who had seen them. He told me those materials had ridden around in the back of his pickup truck for three days, then he decided to hire me. In other words, neither he nor the committee ever looked at them.

I asked him, "Barry, why did you select me without ever reviewing the stuff you asked for?"

He responded unequivocally, "You *did* what you promised!"

He was talking about action.

Is there anything you need to take action on? If so, do it yesterday. But first, let's have a little fun by completing another exercise.

Write down your answer(s) to the question, "What am I putting off to the future that I could address right now?" Then think about the problems that stem from delaying action and the benefits that would come from taking action, and write them down, too.

When we take action, we are choosing the path of Personal Accountability. As a result, we experience the satisfaction and accomplishment—and the control over our own lives—that are so critical to success. We usually move closer to achieving our goals and those of our company. And we feel better about ourselves. It's exciting to slice through organizational inertia, to see the results that come from our achievements and to defeat Procrastination, the Friend of Failure. Action is the partner of productivity and the catalyst for achievement.

Practicing Personal Accountability with the QBQ

Now we've covered all three disciplines for creating a QBQ:

Discipline One: All QBQs begin with "What" or "How," not "Why," "When" or "Who."

Discipline Two: All QBQs contain an "I."

Discipline Three: All QBQs focus on action.

Put the three pieces together and you have a powerful method for practicing Personal Accountability. Is it possible to follow the disciplines and still not have an effective QBQ? Sure. Here are two examples:

"What can I do to make you change?"

"How can I avoid any responsibility in this matter today?"

They fit all the disciplines, but are they QBQs? I sure hope you said, "No!"

My 10-year-old son Michael has a good one too:
"Who can I blame today?"

That one does not even meet the QBQ disciplines! The point is, a QBQ does not consist merely of words. Yes, it is crucial to know and use the three disciplines, but the concepts supporting them are more important: 1) Avoid Victim Thinking, Procrastination and Blame, 2) Remember, "I can only change me!" and 3) Take action!

To help us learn and apply the QBQ, let's contrast some more Incorrect Questions and QBQs to show their differences:

IQ: "When is the customer going to call me back?"

QBQ: "What can I do now to capture his attention?"

IQ: "Why doesn't she help out more?"

QBQ: "How can I serve her today?"

IQ: "Why aren't my people motivated?"

QBQ: "What action can I take to discover what excites each person on the team?"

IQ: "Who failed to give us the information on time?"

QBQ: "How can I contribute today?"

IQ: "Why doesn't he change?"

QBQ: "What can I do to change myself?"

Making the QBQ Personal

Now it's your turn. Can you think of an Incorrect Question you've been asking at work or at home? Write it on a clean sheet of paper. How can you apply Discipline Three, *All QBQs focus on action*, to this question? Check your QBQ to make sure it also reflects Discipline One and Discipline Two:

Discipline One: All QBQs begin with "What" or "How," not "Why," "When" or "Who."

Discipline Two: All QBQs contain an "I."

Now that you have an action-oriented QBQ, you're ready to make a *commitment* to action.

1. Will I take action on my QBQ today?

2. With whom? Where?

3. What will be my purpose?

4. How will I—and they—gain?

Putting Personal Accountability and the QBQ to Work

The advantage of the QBQ is that it's practical. It works because of the three disciplines. When we use it, we're on the road to asking better questions—questions that lead to accountable thinking and action. As we conclude Part 1, look back over these six chapters and reflect on these questions:

1. What point made me think "darn hard"?

2. Which idea did I take issue with and why?

3. If this book were to end here, how would I have changed and what difference would it have made in my organization and my life?

We have a lot more content to explore, but we now have acquired a tool that can change a life. I know, because it has changed mine in many ways for the better. My hope is that we can all put the QBQ into daily practice, both at work and at home. Only then will we capture the amazing rewards that come when we choose the path of Personal Accountability.

Part Two

The Pillar Principles of Prosperity

Introduction

One Saturday morning, I was on a four-lane highway, traveling about 60 miles per hour in a 55-mile-per-hour zone, in the right lane. A state trooper pulled up on my left and looked at me, then drove on. Good, I thought.

Suddenly, he let me take the lead and pulled behind me as we headed down the road, now at exactly 55 mph. By that time, I was starting to think some derogatory thoughts about those who exist "to protect and to serve"!

Then his lights flashed and his siren wailed. I pulled over, hopped from my car and headed back to talk to the guy who was out to ruin my day.

"Good morning, Sir!" I said cheerfully. I was tempted to add, "It's a fine day, Sir, isn't it? You look great today, Sir!" But I kept my mouth shut. He poked his head out his window and said in a deep, gravelly voice, "Morning, Son."

Now, I really didn't like that at all. I was 35 and he was calling me "Son."

Then, chuckling, with half a twinkle in his eye, he said, "Do you always leave an extra set of car keys hanging from your trunk lock?"

I spun around and there they were. My wife's keys were dangling from the trunk, where my daughter had left them that morning. I turned back to face him. Feeling thankful and a bit embarrassed, I smiled and responded, "No, Sir, not normally, Sir. Thank you so much, Sir!"

As he shut his door he yelled, "That's all I wanted! Have a great day!"

Personally, I think he enjoyed every minute of our little encounter.

To the trooper, my keys were obvious. To me, they were not. I might have driven a thousand miles and not noticed them. From behind my car and some distance away he could see them. But I couldn't.

Because I held a negative paradigm, and an incorrect view of the police officer and his purpose for stopping me, my feelings bordered on frustration and anger. I was convinced he was out to get me.

The moment I received new information about the keys, however, all that negativity disappeared in a heartbeat. I suddenly had a new perspective: The trooper was there to help me. In other words, my thinking had changed. That's exactly what Personal Accountability does. When I practice Personal Accountability using the QBQ, I begin to see people and events differently by looking at myself and asking, "What can I do?" and "How can I make a difference?"

Personal Accountability is the key I can't see (or use) until I stop racing down the highway of life and get out and find it. Only then can I take it in hand and use it to unlock a more fulfilling and prosperous life. The QBQ is the tool that helps me do that by eliminating Victim Thinking, Procrastination and Blame.

In Part 1, we have been exploring the concepts of Personal Accountability and the QBQ. In Part 2, we'll explore what I call Pillar Principles of Prosperity. A Pillar Principle is a timeless truth, a rock solid idea on which we can base not only our careers, but also our lives. Leaders in most organizations would agree that these principles are foundational to their success:

Learning	Creativity
Service	Trust
Courage	Clarity
Excellence	Integrity
Ownership	Belief

In my experience with numerous individuals, groups and companies, however, I have noticed that there is little agreement regarding how to develop and consistently practice the behaviors that characterize each of these principles. In Part 2, you will find ideas for making these principles practical in your daily life.

I call them the Pillar Principles of *Prosperity* because to prosper means to grow and thrive. These concepts help each of us grow and thrive in all areas of our lives—professionally, financially, spiritually, emotionally, relationally and intellectually.

The master principle of Personal Accountability provides a solid foundation for the Pillar Principles. It is the key idea upon which the pillars rest, and it is best summed up in one word: *I,* as in, "What can *I* do?"

As we discuss each of the Pillar Principles, we'll show how the QBQ can make that principle "actionable." The QBQ serves as the "how to" tool for practicing the principle every day. Like any tool we can hold in our hand, the QBQ is designed to accomplish an end. As we use it correctly, it enables us to "fix" the unhealthy patterns in our lives by replacing them with more productive ones.

Along the way, we will demonstrate Incorrect Questions (IQs) and model The Question Behind the Question. We will see how IQs prevent us from practicing a certain principle, but QBQs allow us to live out that idea. We will always bear in mind that a better question begins with "What" or "How," not "Why," "When" or "Who." It *always* contains an "I," *never* a "them," "they," "we," "us" or "you." And it focuses on action, because action is the secret to making a positive difference in our own lives, the lives of others and our organizations.

QBQs work. I have observed firsthand what asking more effective questions has done for many people and their organizations. The QBQ serves as a tool for solving problems, improving performance and building relationships while bringing to life the Pillar Principles of Prosperity!

It is my hope that you have great fun exploring, comprehending and applying the Pillar Principles in every area of *your* life. Here we go, together!

Pillar Principle One: Learning

Stacy Enxing Seng works for SCIMED Life Systems, a division of Boston Scientific Corporation. When she was about 12 years old, she and her father, a pilot, took a Sunday afternoon joy ride in a single engine Cessna tail-dragger about a mile in the air over Lake Michigan. Not long into the flight, the joy of their father-daughter adventure came to an abrupt halt when the engine failed.

Stacy's father turned to her and in calm, reassuring tones said: "Honey, the engine has quit. I'm going to need to fly the plane differently."

Interesting phrase, don't you think? Fly the plane differently. Stacy's father had the wisdom to know that changing conditions and new challenges often require different strategies. What works one day in a given situation does not necessarily work the next under different circumstances. Conditions change, markets change, people change. We need to develop a repertoire of responses—strategies and tactics—that allow us to respond when our engines unexpectedly quit.

Stacy's father needed air speed to turn the engine over. He told Stacy he would try to restart the engine by hitting switches in the cockpit while he steered the plane downward toward the deep, cold waters of Lake Michigan. Stacy understood, and, sensing the gravity of the situation, quickly nodded her approval of her dad's plan.

This did not go off to corporate for a committee decision!

Her father sent the plane into a nosedive and fiddled with the switches. He gained air speed, but nothing happened. He leveled off closer to the water. "Stacy, we're going to try that again," he said. "Hang on!" They dove a second time. He hit the switches as the plane gained speed and this time the engine fired, first just a few hopeful sputters. Finally, they heard the secure, familiar hum.

About 20 minutes later, they landed. Then, this Rock of Gibraltar kind of guy, this Fearless Father, this Man of Courage turned to his 12-year-old daughter, lovingly patted her shoulder and said, "Now honey, whatever you do, *don't tell Mom!*"

We will address Courage in a later chapter, but Stacy's father is a good role model for our first Pillar Principle: Learning. Consider the information he processed and the decisions he made in a crisis when his own life and the life of his daughter were at stake. He could have rushed to blame someone for his predicament by asking: "Who built this engine?" He could have postponed these crucial decisions and delayed action by asking: "When is someone going to teach me to handle this changing situation?" Or he could have slipped quickly into Victim Thinking and asked: "Why is this happening to us?"

Had he chosen to dwell on any one of those questions, the outcome could have been tragic. But it wasn't. Stacy's father was committed to Learning. He had the wisdom to plan ahead and learn the procedures for restarting an engine in mid-flight. His preparation, his commitment to Learning and his willingness to adapt to changing conditions allowed him to fly the plane differently—and successfully.

How about you? Whatever your profession, whatever your leadership role, do you need to "fly" your career differently because of the changes you are experiencing?

If so, do you have the knowledge and skills to fly it successfully?

Learning = Change

Too often when confronted with change, we get distracted from Learning because we ask Incorrect Questions such as these:

"Why do we have to go through all this change?"

"When is all this change going to go away?"

"Who's going to support me through this change?"

When we ask these questions, it is clear we are focusing on things beyond our control. They keep us from focusing on the things we can control, our own thinking—and thus our own Learning.

If we succumb to asking those outwardly focused questions, we won't change. Why? Because we won't be investing our time and energy in Learning. Learning requires change. If we don't accept change, Learning will not happen.

To fully embrace the Pillar Principle of Learning, we need to embrace change by conditioning ourselves to ask the QBQs:

"How can I adapt to the changing world?"

"What action can I take today to learn to do one new thing?"

Both questions are constructed well. They follow the guidelines outlined in Part 1. They each begin with "What" or "How," contain an "I" and focus on taking action (They also keep us practicing Personal Accountability!)

One of the challenges we have with Learning is that we don't understand what Learning actually means. We cannot equate Learning with attendance at a three-day program, a national sales meeting or a four-day training workshop. Sometimes we leave a meeting, a class or a training session exclaiming, "Thanks, Boss, loved the speakers, the room temperature was just right and I enjoyed the Danish, too. Oh, by the way, I learned a lot!"

How do we know if we've learned anything? Here's a truth that is fundamental, but it is profound when recognized, understood and practiced:

Learning = Change

When I'm struggling to lose a few pounds, the scales provide the evidence. If I want to sharpen my appearance, a haircut helps and I know I've gotten one simply by looking in the mirror. I know my bench pressing is working if over a period of time the weight I lift goes up.

But how do I know whether I've learned? It's pretty easy, actually. When I can look at a situation that occurs in my life and say: "I used to react differently, but now I respond better," I know I have learned because I have changed.

Merry-Go-Rounds and Roller Coasters

Here's what I've discovered: We all move through change at a different pace. There is no right or wrong speed. One of my clients refers to change as the "change journey," and I hope we're all on one.

When the Millers made the big move from Minneapolis to Denver in late 1997, we experienced a whirlwind weekend looking at about 20 homes in Colorado. By Saturday, I discovered Karen and I were looking at the situation quite differently. I was asking, "Which house should we buy?" and she was asking a more thoughtful question, "Should we move at all?" Feel the difference?

It's true, people move through change at various speeds. Yet, in some organizations, you'd think there was a right way and a wrong way to process change. One executive told me the big problem with his people is that they are "rutted."

"What does 'rutted' mean?" I asked.

"They just aren't changing as fast as I want them to!" The Incorrect Question would be, "Why don't they change as fast as I do?" or "When will they get it?" These QBQs are far more effective: "What can I do differently today?" and "How can I model change?" These questions center my life on the principle of Personal Accountability by directing my energies and efforts toward progressing on my change journey.

Is your world changing? That's certainly a "Duh!" question. For me, there's little point in talking about "all the change." Not many of us need to be told about how fast change is occurring. One way to picture how our environment, and especially our pace, has changed is to imagine life in the mid-1800s. Back then, we might have waited three days for the stagecoach to arrive in our town. Now, we get upset if we miss the next revolution of the bank building's revolving door.

A field rep came up to me at a conference and said, "John, our organization sure has gone through a ton of change. We have a new computer system, a changeover in management, a restructured work force. I've had three supervisors in less than a year!" Before I could comment, she blurted out in a defensive tone, "I really don't mind change, John, *but just not all at once!*"

Sometimes change does seem to happen all at once. But as long as we focus on the changing world and not on ourselves, we'll just waste precious time and energy, while creating stress. One thing I've become convinced of is this: I can change. You can change. People change all the time, but each person changes at a unique pace.

In the Steve Martin movie "Parenthood," the grandmother gave Steve's character and his wife this sage advice (paraphrased): Some people see life as a merry-go-round and others see life as a roller coaster. Some like it calm and unchanging and some are unhappy unless change is taking them over the highest heights and through the deepest dives. Neither perspective is good or bad—it is just a perspective.

Change is Here to Stay

The key to acting on the Pillar Principle of Learning is to acknowledge and accept change. It's one of life's true constants.

Tom Clifford, a vice president with Norwest, will tell you successful business people need to adapt continually to changing conditions. Case in point: Tom's 14-year-old son, Brandon, was given a research assignment in ninth grade history class. He was to produce a report on an obscure German mathematician. Drawing on his own educational experience, Tom cautioned his son: "You'd better get down to the library and get some books if you're going to complete that project on time."

Predictably, Brandon replied: "Don't sweat it, Pop. I've got lots of time."

Tom assumed his son was procrastinating. Maybe he was. But the night before the project was due, the boy logged on to the Internet at home, found plenty of information on "this German dude" and produced a report that earned him an excellent grade—and taught Tom something, too.

"People are going to have a tough time competing with Brandon in 10 years," Tom told me.

I thought perhaps this was just a proud father talking, but then he made a key point, a lesson for those of us in the corporate world about change and adapting to a changing environment.

"John, when we need to get things done around here," Tom said, "a project gets assigned and people sometimes respond, 'Two weeks?! I can't get that done in two weeks! I need more time.' Well, the 24-year-old will know how to get it done in two days or two hours because the tools of technology will have been a part of his life since he was six!"

I understood. Adapt or crash, just like Stacy and her dad.

Reducing the Drag

The book *The Fifth Discipline* by Peter Senge describes how organizational systems evolve and adapt. Senge coined the now-popular phrase, "learning organization." But do organizations really learn? Of course not. People learn. Individuals change. They move the organization forward.

I'd like to counter with the term "learning organism" and apply it to the lifelong-learning available to all individuals. We can all be learning organisms if we remember that school is life and life is school. If we claim to be a learning organism, though, we need to know *what* changes when we learn. Naturally, the end product we seek is better results flowing from new behaviors. New practices are what we're after. But before that, we'd better change something else.

All organizations have something George Barr of Cenex-Land O' Lakes calls "cultural drag." Have you ever observed Olympic swimmers and noticed how little body hair they have? It's practically non-existent, because swimmers shave to reduce the potential friction, or drag, their hair causes in the water.

Likewise, organizations and individuals can improve their performance when they reduce their drag. For organizations, the cultural drag is the old thinking to which people cling. Its presence often is evidenced by the Seven Sinful Words: "We've never done it that way before."

When we eliminate that statement from our organization's conversation and instead start asking, "How can I apply this new idea?" we've changed our thinking and reduced the drag. Then we can claim Learning.

We ourselves often create the most drag on our Learning because we aren't able to see and nurture the potential within.

Discovering the Angel

Do you talk to yourself? When I ask that question in a live presentation, about half the group raises their hands to affirm that they do. The rest sit there thinking, "I don't know, do I talk to myself? Nah, there's no way I talk to myself."

People talk to themselves all day, and even all night long. Dr. Alfred Adler called this self-talk our "private logic." We argue with ourselves and defend our positions as we attempt to justify what we do, where we go, who we are.

My self-talk is my thinking and, in order to learn, I need to identify and change what I say to myself. Are you aware of what you're saying to yourself? I hope so, because it determines in large part whether you succeed or fail.

Michaelangelo stated, "I saw the angel in the marble and I chiseled until I set it free."

Imagine if you were able to look at a block of unfinished, virgin material and see the potential locked inside. You get a close-up look at unfinished material every morning when you look in the mirror. It's you, CEO of Self.

I once read that the average human being goes to the grave having tapped only 10 percent of the brain's potential. Wouldn't it be great to be above average and get that figure up to maybe 12 percent? Wouldn't it be terrific at the end of our lives to be able to say, "I only wasted 88 percent of my potential instead of 90 percent like everyone else!"?

Oliver Wendell Holmes summed it up best: "What lies behind us and what lies before us pale in significance to what lies *within* us."

It is possible to capture more of our potential if we change our thinking, change the way we view our world and change the way we talk to ourselves about ourselves. Then we are practicing the Pillar Principle of Learning.

When I look in the mirror, do I see the angel within the marble?

Am I at least chiseling in the right direction?

Am I, through my self-talk, giving myself good advice about change, about Learning and about reaching my potential? If not, I need to pick up the chisel and get to work.

You Can Get There from Here

After 10,000 hours of conducting interactive training sessions with organizations and group of all kinds, I have come to understand that there are always roadblocks that get in the way of Learning. And guess what? Most of them are of our own construction. They are embodied in the poisonous, negative self-talk that too often defeats us before we even begin.

Over time, I've been able to identify six common Roadblocks to Learning. They center around excuses, ill-founded expectations, a sense of entitlement, closed minds, selective perception and fatigue. The good news is that we are in control of each of them, because each is related to how we think and how we talk to ourselves. Once identified, these Roadblocks can be neutralized. The individual, the learning organism, takes charge. With each Roadblock to Learning we eliminate from our minds, we change our thinking, which leads to permanent and positive change. Only by eliminating these Roadblocks can we practice the Pillar Principle of Learning.

Roadblock to Learning One

The Exception Excuse: "This material looks pretty good, but it can't possibly apply to me." Translation: I'm the exception!

Dale Dauten, a syndicated newspaper columnist who refers to himself as the Corporate Curmudgeon, wrote, "Confidence is believing you have something to teach; arrogance is believing you have nothing to learn."

Even a well-educated, seasoned professional stops growing and learning if he or she allows the Exception Excuse to take root. The man who showed the slide that read: "*Personal* Accountability Begins With YOU!" had a case of this disease.

A Tale of Two CEOs

Let me tell you about two CEOs and how differently they approach this Pillar Principle of Learning.

Michael Wigley is the CEO of Great Plains Supply, a farm and home-improvement supply retailer and a successful firm by any measure. Mike has a degree from Harvard and for a time served as a management consultant. One of the principles he and his team use as a guide is, "Be open to the 1 percent possibility."

In our initial meeting, I asked Mike to explain that principle to me. He said his firm was having a terrific year. Profits were up. Earnings were up. People wanted to work for the company. It was buying up its competitors. This was a positive picture and a very seductive one. The company easily could become smug and step out of the learning posture. By remaining open to the 1 percent possibility, though, Mike and his team are able to avoid the Exception Excuse Roadblock.

"We must never get to the point where we think we know it all," Mike says. "So we constantly keep in mind there's *at least* a 1 percent possibility that we can do things better."

He was saying that advancement does not equal arrival. Sometimes we pretend we're too successful to learn more. We all need to keep coming up with better ideas, and being smug or unaware of possibilities limits our potential for continued success.

If you think you've "arrived," or if I begin to think I'm a "finished product" and have reached my destination, then I have one word for both of us: Titanic! Because that's where human arrogance met the unknown. The more successful we are, if we're not careful, the easier it can be for our egos to capsize even the most impressive accomplishments.

Is it possible to forget that we don't know what we don't know? As Joel Barker, the futurist, says, be careful not to suffer from the "terminal disease of certainty"! That's what Michael Wigley was talking about. Let's be open to the 1 percent (or 10 percent or 20 percent) possibility that we can do things differently—and better.

This poem sums up the principle in a different way:

Here lies the body of Jonathan J.,
who died maintaining the right of way.
He was right—dead right—as he rode along,
but just as dead as if he had been wrong!

Our second CEO, Tim, didn't subscribe to the 1 percent possibility. He seemed to be a learned man, about 50, fully capable of running a $40 million printing company. About the time he invited me to provide training for his staff, I was reading Peter Senge's book *The Fifth Discipline*, about the learning organization. Since the book was loaded with great ideas that could benefit any culture, I thought Tim might enjoy it, and I gave it to him as a gift.

In preparation for the training, I interviewed his vice presidents to discover their opinions on the critical issues facing the business. What they said stunned me. Tim was a horrible communicator. There was no corporate vision. Confusion reigned. The manufacturing floor was about to go union. Nobody felt they knew Tim. Essentially, there was no Trust, a Pillar Principle we'll explore later.

I swallowed hard and returned to Tim with my findings. I decided to ease into what would be a difficult conversation by asking him what he thought of Senge's book.

I'll never forget his response. He reached back to his credenza, grabbed *The Fifth Discipline*, handed it to me and calmly stated: "It was OK, but it really didn't have much application to us."

I couldn't believe my ears. The Exception Excuse had become a major barrier for Tim, and thus for the organization. Six months later, the board of directors asked him to resign.

Let's make sure we never become so blinded by what's happening in our own world that we let the Exception Excuse become a Roadblock to Learning. It never will if we commit to Personal Accountability and continue to ask the QBQ, "How can I apply these ideas today?"

Roadblock to Learning Two

The Expectations Dilemma: "I'll bet this won't be any good."

It's difficult to expand a closed mind. I was talking with my neighbor over the back fence one day. He told me how he had endured a recent three-day training session offered by his company. He described it as boring, irrelevant and a waste of time. He capped off his caustic review with these telltale words: "I wasn't surprised. *I knew it wouldn't be any good.*"

We often find what we are looking for. We get what we expect. This happens when we enter a potential learning situation expecting the worst. Those expectations flow from our preconceived notions, which are based, in part, on our training experiences and on our own Roadblocks to Learning.

We are our own worst enemies. Our self-talk limits us by arguing there is nothing to gain, nothing to learn and no changes worth making. Do you think my neighbor gave that training session and his own Learning a fighting chance? Not when he had already convinced himself going in that it would be boring, irrelevant and a waste of time.

Then there are people like Doug Lennick, executive vice president of American Express Financial Advisors. He once told me: "My opportunities to learn far exceed the times I actually do so." He recognizes that what he gets out of a learning opportunity is directly related to what he puts into it. And if our expectations are not based on asking, "What can I take away and apply today?" we won't take away very much.

Roadblock to Learning Three

The Experience Exclusion: "When am I going to hear something new?"

Bill Tevendale, a VP with State Farm, observes, "It's a funny thing. When you ask people who only care about their tenure, what they do, they report, 'Well, I've been around this organization for X number of years!' But the leaders who are concerned with being effective will talk to you about what they're *accomplishing.*"

Experience and tenure should be our window to understanding. But our experience also can be an impediment to Learning. Experience ceases to be an asset when our self-talk excludes new ideas because we believe we already know all there is to know because we have "X years of experience."

Mark Twain said he never had much time for experts. They never wanted to add to what they already knew. "If there ever was more to learn, then they wouldn't be expert no more," he said.

Exclusion from Learning is an automatic result of asking, "Haven't we heard this before?" So what if we have? Shouldn't we be asking the QBQ, "What can I do to apply what I'm hearing?" That would do away with the Experience Exclusion Roadblock.

Let's face it. Nobody is inventing new truths. Truth itself doesn't change. But by discovering and practicing the truths that already exist, we can change ourselves and experience the Pillar of Learning. The old stuff is probably the good stuff. Seeing, understanding and abiding by truths are what's important. There are truths worth learning, and they're embodied in the salesperson who shows a heartfelt concern for the customer, the manager who lifts people up rather than tears them down, the executive who gets out from behind the desk and talks to the people.

Let's never ask the IQ, "When am I going to hear something new?" Some great ideas may seem new to us, but in reality, principles that work can be so old they're new to the person hearing them. The QBQ may be a new acronym to you, but the truth of Personal Accountability is not only timely but timeless.

I had just finished speaking on Personal Accountability to about 800 people in Seattle, when an older gentleman with pure white hair shook my hand and said, "Young man, I sure wish somebody had said those things to me 30 years ago."

I appreciated the compliment, but a wave of sadness washed over me. Did this man believe his long career had been wasted? Was he saying he was giving up?

I responded with a chuckle and said: "Well, how old are you, young man?"

"Sixty-two," came his response. Then he added, "And it's never too late. I'm going to use this stuff." He wasn't going to let his experience be a Roadblock to his Learning—even at age 62.

Roadblock to Learning Four

The Entitlement Disease: "When am I going to get what I deserve?"

I was in the cafeteria of a client corporation once and there on the wall, from our government, was a statement that, if taken literally, makes dependents of us all. "You are entitled to ... ." It then lists the pay, benefits and privileges due employees. I'm sure the assumption is that employees perform their part of the contract, and then the company is required to meet its part of the bargain. But the poster doesn't say this.

Salaries, commissions, wages and benefits are not entitlements; they're commitments based upon an exchange of value, whether it's phrased as work for pay or pay for work. That's not what the sign says, however.

Judith M. Bardwick, in her best-selling book *Danger in the Comfort Zone* hits the nail on the head. The book's subtitle reads: "From Boardroom to Mailroom—How to Break the Entitlement Habit That's Killing American Business." That neatly summarizes her main thesis and provides a keen insight into an extremely relevant business issue.

The self-talk of the entitled is: "I have a right to an education." "Pay for my schooling." "You owe me a job." Have you heard these demands? "Where's my 4 percent annual merit increase? I've been here for six months already." What these complainants are missing is the other half of the conversation that speaks to the contractual nature of the work relationship: Salaries, commissions and wages are paid as an exchange for services performed. We are entitled to them when we have held up our end of the contract—in other words, when we have *earned* them.

A leader named Bob Herman understands this. After almost 25 years with 3M and its spin-off, Imation, he told me, "I've always viewed my relationship with the organization as a year-to-year 'contract.' I do my job and I'm rewarded, but every January 1, my contract starts over."

At times, I fail to exercise the principle of Personal Accountability because I succumb to the mind-set that I deserve things simply for trying hard or putting in long hours or making repeated attempts to accomplish a goal. I've come to believe, however, that I don't deserve a sale just because I've worked hard. If I didn't make the sale, I didn't make the sale! I simply was unable to get the prospect to believe in what I was offering. It is only when I deliver the value I've committed to deliver that I earn the agreed-upon rewards.

Have you ever had the privilege of playing Tooth Fairy? When our daughter, Tara, was 12, she came to me with a tooth in her hand. I couldn't believe it. Another one? I was seeing dollar signs and wondering, "When does this end?"

I recovered enough to do a little teasing and teaching. "You know, honey, what you've got to do is put that tooth under your pillow tonight and, if you're lucky, you might get something."

She looked at me as if I had missed a memo. As she stuck out her hand she said, "Dad, give me a break and give me a buck."

Hers was an entitlement stance. She believed she had something coming and she wanted it now. That's probably to be expected in a young child. But when that same mind-set persists into adulthood, it poses another Roadblock to Learning.

If we ask most people, "Who's accountable for the thoughts in your brain right now?" they will tell the truth: "I am." If we ask, "Who's accountable for your 'personal development'?" they still say, "I am." But, if the question is altered ever so slightly and we inquire, "Who's accountable for your *training?*" guess how people tend to answer? That's right, through code talk, they say, "Somebody other than me!" The manager, the human resource department, the field trainer, the marketing people who wrote the product syllabus, my company, the seminar speaker, my parents, the coach, the world around me!

Two Who Invested in Learning

Rich Chapian got into sales at 23 and did he ever sell! Quickly, he sold his motorcycle, his car, his furniture and his house. He was selling everything he owned to pay the bills until he realized that having a great personality does not mean you will have success in sales. He wasn't selling what his company hired him to sell, and he knew he needed help.

He went to his brother-in-law and did something a lot of us probably wouldn't do: He borrowed $800. Why? Because his company was not offering professional sales training. Nevertheless, he didn't sit around with the Entitlement Disease. He asked a better question, the QBQ, "What can I do to develop myself?" and he took that $800 and invested it in himself by purchasing the Dale Carnegie sales training course. That's Personal Accountability.

Rich learned to sell and by age 35 was the CEO and owner of a very profitable company. His personal growth and development preceded his success, and preceding the personal growth was his not waiting for someone to hand him anything on a platter.

Do I believe organizations should invest in the development of their greatest asset, people? Yes. But I also believe, in the final analysis, you and I are accountable for our own personal change journey. If the training you need is not being offered, go get it. Be like Rich, who was able to repay his brother-in-law with interest!

Years after the Dale Carnegie sales training, I called Rich and was told he was away for two weeks at a leadership development conference.

Since he was the president and CEO of his company, do you think someone sent him? Yes, somebody did. He sent himself. In some ways Rich is a rare leader, but there are other people who don't have the Entitlement Disease, and they are making a difference in the lives of others. Let me tell you about another.

David excitedly approached me after a talk at his travel company and asked, "Mr. Miller, do you have a book?" "No, not yet, David, but I will some day. Why do you ask?" "Oh, if I just had some way to review your material, I could apply it better!" I thanked him and told him when it was out I'd send him a copy. We parted, but his question left an impression on me. It had nothing to do with John Miller. It had everything to do with his internal desire to learn, change and grow.

After we spoke, I followed David's group into another room for lunch and the annual awards banquet. I watched the regional vice president get up and laud the people who had achieved, invite them to come forward for their rewards and send them to their seats smothered in applause. Finally, it was time for the "Top Agent of the Year" announcement and celebration. As an outsider, I could sense the importance of this award and could see the anticipation on the faces of those who hoped to receive it. It was to go to the person who not only produced impressive revenues for the company, but who also possessed those intangible qualities of leadership. The RVP built up the appropriate suspense. Then the name was given. We stood. We cheered. Who do you think it was?

David.

I will go to my grave convinced there is a direct correlation between David's question to me—essentially, "Do you have a resource so I can keep learning and improving?"—and the fact that he was the region's top achiever. It wasn't luck, height, heritage, family background or good looks. It was the need and desire continually to earn the right to serve others. That's the antithesis of the Entitlement Disease. And it only comes from asking the QBQ, "What can I do today to develop *myself?*" and "How can I improve *myself?*"

Whenever we begin asking someone else to take care of our training or our personal development, we've jumped the track. We're blocking out our own ability to change through Learning, because we're now carrying the cancerous thoughts of the Entitlement Disease.

The danger of the Entitlement Disease is that it moves us further away from Personal Accountability. We stop looking inward for the answers to our success and start assigning that task to others. Our growth and development—our Learning—is our own responsibility.

Roadblock to Learning Five

Execution Habit: "I don't like the messenger, so I won't hear the message."

Have you ever shot the messenger? I have. After I finished a talk in front of 300 salespeople in Des Moines, I came down from the platform to shake hands. Personally, I thought it was one of the best presentations I'd ever delivered. The response from those around me seemed to confirm that.

As the excitement died down, I noticed one person still in the ballroom whose face told me she was "underwhelmed." She was the one who coordinated the meeting. I certainly wanted her opinion. After a little coaxing, she critiqued me. She said there was something about my style of delivery that distracted her. She simply did not like it.

I smiled and thanked her for her candor. But let me tell you what I was really thinking. It's not pretty, but it's real. "What do you know? You're not a salesperson or a speaker. You're a meeting planner."

In my mind, I had executed her. By eroding her credentials, I marginalized her and I was able to dismiss her criticism because she couldn't possibly understand what it's like to do what I do. But do you know what? She was right. She shared an insight that, when I decided later to apply it, helped me communicate a great deal better with the audience.

I've seen this happen hundreds of times. Consider the salesperson who dismisses what the marketing person says because, "He's never been in the field." How about the manufacturing person who shoots down the vice president of sales because, "You and your people get all the perks and we do all the work." Or the executive who doesn't listen to the administrative assistant because, "Well, what could she possibly know?"

It's easy to miss learning opportunities because of this habit of executing the messenger. But it's a mistake—a mistake we can avoid if we continue to ask the QBQ: "How can I listen with an open mind and apply what this person has to say?"

Roadblock to Learning Six

The Exhaustion Quagmire: "Why is this happening to me?"

Stress is a choice, and when we make the wrong choice, the Pillar of Learning—the natural fuel for change—is lost.

Change and stress often occur at the same time. But this does not mean that change causes stress. It all depends on how we choose to react to the stress. Anger, hostility, defensiveness and an inability to make decisions lead to our failure to deal constructively with the stressors in our lives. It is not the stressor that causes distress. It's our thinking. It's us.

I remember seeing an interview with Alan Simpson, the retired US Senator, on television. The interviewer asked him, "Hasn't being a Senator all these years been tremendously stressful for you?"

He replied: "Well, I suspect milking cows would be stressful if you made it that way."

He's right. Too often we try to control the uncontrollable, stop the unstoppable and change the unchangeable. The minute we try to do that we have made a choice that brings us distress. It is a choice that keeps us from learning and leads us to exhaustion.

For instance, one cold winter evening as I was heading out of downtown Minneapolis, my tire blew. I pulled to the side of the road and reached for my cell phone to call the motor club. The problem was that the cell phone was home warm and safe on the kitchen counter.

I stepped out of my car into an icy wind and finally hailed a passing state highway vehicle. The two men inside were only too happy to help a man dressed in his finest suit change a tire. After I thanked these Good Samaritans and watched their taillights fade into the Minnesota night, I went to start my car. Nothing happened. The battery was dead. I'd left the lights on too long while we changed the flat.

My first impulse was to scream in frustration an IQ such as, "Why is this happening to me?" But then I remembered that I couldn't alter the circumstances. What happened, happened. I'll never forget looking to the heavens with my arms outstretched and almost yelling my self-talk: "Stress is a choice!"

A fatigued, drained disposition does not promote Learning. But the minute we let go of what we cannot change and control, distress dissipates, and we can begin to learn, change and grow! For that to happen, we need to ask this question, which just may be the ultimate QBQ:

"What can I do today to let go of that which I cannot control?"

And isn't that most everything but ourselves?

Stress is a choice. I first taught that concept at a medical device company. I was finished speaking and a woman in her mid-twenties rushed up and, breaking all the rules of political correctness we've developed in the corporate world, gave me a big hug. She then introduced herself as Jenny, a district sales manager from Georgia, the Atlanta market. She explained how the new thought—that she was creating her own stress, which was holding her back from being more effective—would change her life. I asked her to send me a note letting me know how she used it. One month later, the note came.

Without going into great detail, I can tell you she ceased trying to halt the changing environment in the ever-evolving medical business. She also stopped trying to change her boyfriend and control her sales reps. Plainly put, she saved her energy for something else: changing herself through Learning. She was no longer mentally, physically and emotionally exhausted from attempting to do the inhuman! She'd pulled herself from that quagmire by ceasing and desisting from asking the IQ, "Why is this happening to me?"

Remember, it's not the stressor that causes the distress. It's our thinking. It's our stubborn desire to change the unchangeable that causes us to sink into the Exhaustion Quagmire. And that's when our Learning stops.

Making Learning Personal

Here are the Roadblocks to Learning from this section:

One – **The Exception Excuse:** "This material looks pretty good, but it can't possibly apply to me!"

Two – **The Expectations Dilemma:** "I'll bet this isn't going to be any good."

Three – **The Experience Exclusion:** "When am I going to hear something new?"

Four – **The Entitlement Disease:** "When am I going to get what I deserve?"

Five – **The Execution Habit:** "I don't like the messenger, so I won't hear the message."

Six – **The Exhaustion Quagmire:** "Why is this happening to me?"

Some questions for personal reflection:

1. Of the six Roadblocks to Learning, which one do I need to eliminate from my life?

2. How much more productive and innovative can I be as a learning organism when I remove the Roadblocks?

3. What will that do for my organization?

4. If Learning equals change, how must I change so I can claim I have learned?

5. What action will I take today to carry out the Pillar Principle of Learning in my own life?

Pillar Principle Two: Service

Michael DeVito is a friend and client who lives in Minneapolis. For several months, Michael and some friends had been planning a March camping trip to Mt. Marcy, the highest peak in the Adirondacks. The Wednesday before the weekend they were going, Michael was in Chicago when he suddenly realized he had forgotten one very important detail: boots.

This trip promised to be cold and wet, making a decent pair of boots a dire necessity. Michael had meant to order a new pair but here he was, out of town two days before the trip, with no boots.

He called information and got L.L. Bean's 800-number. The woman who answered identified herself as Kristi. "Kristi, I don't have a catalog with me, but I'm looking for a pair of boots I meant to order a month ago. I saw them in the catalog, so I know you have them."

She laughed genuinely and said, "We only have about 120 types of boots to offer you, Sir! Let's see if we can narrow it down a bit." Michael sensed he was in good hands.

The transaction turned into a friendly conversation as Michael told Kristi what he was planning, the weather he expected, and the terrain he'd be hiking. From this information, she concluded he probably wanted a pair of "cold weather" boots, which whittled the possibilities down to a more manageable dozen pairs or so. Michael then described every detail he could remember from the catalog, and between the two of them, they pinpointed three possibilities. They were almost there.

Then Kristi asked, "When did you want them?"

Somewhat embarrassed, Michael confessed, "To be honest with you, I need them this Friday afternoon. The trip is this weekend."

Kristi took a moment to think. Then she said, "Normally we ship two-day UPS and I can't get them out until tomorrow, which is Thursday. So that won't work for us at all, will it?" she asked rhetorically.

Michael, who was starting to lose hope, added, "And we don't even know which boots I need."

Then Kristi saved the day. "Here's what I'll do, Michael. Tomorrow, I'll over-night a pair of each of the three types of boots in your size. You'll get them Friday. Try them all on and pick out the pair you want, then ship the others back. I'll include a return shipment ticket, all filled out. You just call the UPS number on it and they'll come to your door and pick up the pairs you don't want. Meanwhile, give me your credit card number, and I won't charge anything to it until you call me Monday and tell me which ones you took on your trip. Would this plan be workable for you?"

Long Pause.

"Michael, Michael, are you there? Would that be all right with you?"

After a few moments of stunned silence, Michael finally responded, "OK!"

As Michael told me that story, I could see in his eyes that he wasn't just talking about a company that had met his needs, or even about a person who had gone beyond all expectations. He was sharing an experience he could still feel fully three years after the fact—one he would never forget.

When I finally asked him how the camping trip went, he laughed and said, "I don't remember. I spent the whole weekend raving to 12 guys about L.L. Bean!"

What a great story! That's the kind of difference our second Pillar Principle, Service, can make. Not only was Michael understandably thrilled, but from that moment on, he would tell that story every chance he got. A company can't *buy* that kind of advertising!

I received Service like that once too, not from Kristi, but from Jacob.

Whether We Offer It or Not

Have you ever been to a Rock Bottom Brewery? It's a chain of restaurants based in Denver. I met Jacob one day when I was in their Minneapolis location for lunch. I didn't have much time and they were busy that day, but they had a seat at the bar available so I was seated right away. I was happy about that, but after a few minutes I still hadn't been waited on and I was starting to get concerned. Just then, a young man ran by me carrying dirty dishes on a tray and noticed me out of the corner of his eye. He stopped, came back and said, "Sir, have you been helped?"

"No, I haven't been," I replied, relieved, "but all I really want is a salad and a couple of rolls."

"I can get you that, Sir. What would you like to drink?"

"I'll have a Diet Coke, please."

"Oh, I'm sorry, Sir, we only sell Pepsi. Would that be all right?"

"Ah, no thanks," I said with a smile, "I'll just have water. That'll be fine."

"Great, I'll be back." He disappeared.

Moments later he came back with the salad, the bread and the water.

"Thank you," I said.

"You're welcome, Sir," he said, and off he went again.

I was enjoying my meal when suddenly I saw a blur of activity off to my left. The "winds of enthusiasm" stirred behind me. Then, over my shoulder stretched the "long arm of Service," delivering a 20-ounce bottle, frosty on the outside, cold on the inside. It was—you guessed it—Diet Coke. "Wow, thank you!" I exclaimed.

"You're welcome," Jacob said with a smile as he hurried off again.

Hey! Wait a minute, I thought. Something extraordinary just happened here. My mind was filled with questions, and as soon as I could get his attention, I motioned him to the bar.

"Excuse me, I thought you didn't sell Coke?" I asked.

"That's right, Sir, we don't."

"Well, where did this come from?"

"The grocery store around the corner, Sir."

I was taken aback. "Who paid for it?" I asked.

"I did, Sir; just a dollar," he replied proudly.

By then I was thinking profound thoughts such as, Wow! This is really cool.

I thought about this marvelous gesture for a moment and then said, "You've been awfully busy. How did you have time to go get it?"

Seemingly growing taller before my eyes, he said, "I didn't, Sir. *I sent my manager.*"

I couldn't believe it. Is that empowerment or what? I'll bet we all can think of times we would love to look at our managers and say, "Get me a Diet Coke!" What a great image!

Pointing at the cold drink, I looked up at Jacob and asked what turned out to be the naïve question of the month, "Why?"

He looked at me, puzzled, then delivered a complete customer Service program in the form of one simple question. He asked, "Pardon me, Sir, maybe I was mistaken. Didn't you want one?"

What a novel idea. Wish I had paper and pen so I could write that down, I thought. Get the customers exactly what they want and need, *whether we offer it or not.*

That was great Service. Actually, it was better than great—it was exceptional. And that's the kind of Service people want.

The Exception to the Rule

Unfortunately though, Service such as Jacob's and Kristi's *is* the exception. For that matter, more and more, even good Service seems to be the exception to the rule. More often we have experiences such as this next one.

The dry cleaners delivered to my house a shirt I was pretty sure was not mine. How did I figure that out? It was light pink with ruffles and sequins down the front. I called the cleaners to say I had someone else's cleaning. The person who answered the phone said, "How do you know it's not your shirt, Mr. Miller?"

"Well," I said, "first of all, it's pink with ruffles and sequins." Not seeming to understand the significance of that, she instructed me to turn the collar inside out. I obliged and said, "OK, so?"

"Do you see a label there?" she asked.

"Yes I do," I assured her.

"And is there a name written there in black pen?" she interrupted. "Yes, there is, but ... ."

Again, she broke in, "Mr. Miller, would you please read the name to me?"

I went along, not sure how to stop her. "It says John Miller, but ... ." Again, my words were cut short as she concluded, like a prosecuting attorney proud to have won her case, "Well, Mr. Miller, I guess that proves it—it's your shirt!"

I have to admit, that story still makes me laugh. But I never used that dry cleaners again. And there's the price we pay for giving bad Service: We lose customers. It happens every day with all kinds of customers.

A Customer is a Customer is a Customer

I have a friend named Chris Wallace who sold insurance for a company based in Des Moines, Iowa. I consider Chris a man of real principle. He told me of a time when he provided a client with a sizable life insurance policy that netted Chris a $4,000 commission check.

Now, if you've ever been in sales, how does it feel to make a sale like that? Grrreat! Right? And how does it feel to *lose* a sale? Ouch! To say it hurts is an understatement.

Well, the new policy holder called Chris shortly afterward and cancelled his policy. You can imagine the disappointment Chris must have felt at having to give up those commission dollars, not to mention losing a potential long-term client relationship.

Dejected, Chris called the home office to cancel the policy and get a check kicked out for the customer. He also needed to have the commission withdrawn from his account. He reached somebody in operations and explained the situation and what needed to be done. The response? "Sorry but I don't know if my computer will let me do that. Can you call back on Monday?"

Do you think Chris felt well served? I can tell you he didn't, and that's one of the reasons he no longer works for the organization. Chris wasn't a customer in the classic sense, but he was certainly Someone who needed Service and when he didn't get it, the company lost him too.

I can just hear you thinking, "Aha! Chris is an *internal customer!*"

I say that because I've been through the same sessions you have, in which the facilitator guides the group in listing on a flip chart all the external customers in one column and all the internal customers in another.

Typically, external customers are people who purchase, consume and benefit from our products and services—policy holders for insurance, hungry people for restaurants. Internal customers are people inside the organization, such as Chris, who serve each other in various ways. The idea is, of course, that we should start thinking of and serving our internal customers the same way we do our external customers. Had Chris' company done that, things might have turned out much differently.

Adding the internal customer label can definitely make a difference. My only problem is that I don't believe it goes far enough. I suggest we forget the flip charts and labels altogether, because if we want to truly bring the Pillar of Service to life, those labels are too limiting.

In fact, there may be lots of other people in your life you would have considered unlikely customers—until now, I hope. In an earlier chapter, I mentioned that my wife Karen and I spent some valuable time working with a marriage counselor, Terry. In one particularly frank session, Terry got our attention with a comment that went straight to our hearts:

"You two had better get your act together, because you've got four little customers at home who are counting on you!"

That hurt! But he was right. It's true, our kids really *are* our customers. We serve them in different ways from the ways we serve our business customers, but we serve them just the same. And who deserves excellent Service more than those in our own families?

So now we have yet another category of customers. Does that mean we need another flip chart? And where does it stop? Friends? Pets? Cars? Instead of making things ever more complicated, it seems to me we'd be better off just to change the definition of a customer.

The 360-Degree Customer Concept

Terry taught us a great lesson that day. And that lesson helped me create what I believe is a much better definition of a customer. I call it "The 360-Degree Customer Concept," and it's very practical. It simply says this:

A customer is anyone who has a legitimate expectation of me

Labeling people may help us serve some of them better initially, but it also invariably leaves others out. Let's just do away with all of the labels and remember a new answer to this QBQ: "What can I do today to serve those who deserve my best?" Of course, that's everyone who has legitimate expectations of me!

I was visiting with Howard Bergerud, owner of both the Nicollet Island Inn in Minneapolis and the Lowell Inn in Stillwater, Minnesota—two of the area's most unique and enjoyable places to stay.

Howard told me an interesting story about a time Bill Cosby was staying at the Nicollet Island Inn. It seems Mr. Cosby is partial to Evian water. That posed no problem, of course, especially since it was for "Mr. Huxtable" himself. But he also has a specific preference for Evian in *glass* bottles, as opposed to the usual plastic bottles that can be found most anywhere.

One of Howard's leaders, a person committed to Service, went to work. Like a bloodhound on a promising trail, she searched the Twin Cities. She called every grocery store in the phone book, from the biggest chain to the smallest Mom-and-Pop store. Finally, some 30 miles away, she discovered a treasure-trove of Evian in glass bottles. Eureka! The troops rejoiced, someone went to retrieve the treasure, and Mr. Cosby got what he wanted.

Impressed and inspired by her story of "going the extra mile," I said to Howard, "She's a keeper! Wasn't that great Service?"

You know what he said—this man who's been in the hospitality field for so many years? "You're right, John, we sure want to keep her. But in reality, great Service would be if she would go to the same effort for *any* guest staying with us."

Good point, Howard. Good point. The true spirit of Service, as exemplified in the 360-Degree Customer Concept, says that everyone deserves our best.

Some people have resisted this idea. A director of marketing at a sizeable firm once said, "I'm not sure I can embrace your definition of a customer, John!"

"Oh?" I probed.

"Yes. I mean, if we start treating the end users of our products the way we've treated our internal people we're going to have a real problem on our hands!" I'll bet they already had a problem.

I've also heard these rebuttals: "Well, who defines 'legitimate'?" and "Everybody?! John, did I hear you right?" and "I accept this approach for this and that group (or person), but not for them, him or her!"

Now, I didn't call it the 192-Degree or 287-Degree Customer Concept, but the 360-Degree Customer Concept. This means we serve the customers *all around us:* everybody we come in contact with, all day long, in every area of our lives, in every role we play.

Is the hotel's housekeeper my customer? How about the cashier scanning my groceries? The flight attendant giving me safety instructions? The guy who picks up my dry-cleaning? Is he my customer? You bet he is. They all are. Why? Because they all have legitimate expectations of me.

Fortunately, the negative responses are in the minority. Most people seem to embrace this concept easily, even instinctively. After a QBQ talk in Cleveland, for example, I received an e-mail from a manufacturing plant manager who wrote, "Using the 360-Degree Customer

Concept, John, I see the world today with *new eyes!* No longer do I see 'my people' but 'my customers' all around me *inside* the plant! Because of this change in my paradigm, I will be a better leader." And he's right. He will be a better leader.

To fully bring the Pillar of Service into our lives, I believe we must first start to look at the world around us with new eyes, and see that virtually everyone in our lives justifiably can be seen as a customer. We can then use the QBQ and Personal Accountability to help us practice this Pillar. We can then truly serve.

Service with a QBQ

Let's look again at the Jacob story. It was a busy lunch hour and he noticed a customer who wasn't even sitting in his section, but he took it upon himself to do what he could anyway. Whether he used the words or not, his actions clearly indicated accountable thinking such as, "What can I do right now to make a difference?" and "How can I provide value to you?" His thinking and his actions made all the difference in the world.

I share Jacob's story wherever I go and I'm frequently amazed at the impact it has on others. Long after a talk, people will remember, comment on and, most importantly, emulate Jacob. In the Pillar Principle of Clarity, we'll talk about one such person, a leader who refocused on his mission by focusing on Jacob's heart for Service. So without even knowing it, Jacob, at just 22 years of age, has become a Service Hero for people all over the country.

But there's another hero in the story, isn't there? Absolutely. It's Jacob's manager. Think about this: Jacob ran to his manager and said, "Hey, would you get this guy a Diet Coke?"

What did his manager say? "Yes!" But more excitingly, what *didn't* she say? She didn't come back with one of these responses:

"Wait a minute Jake, who works for whom here, anyway?"

"Well, I don't know, what have you done for me lately?"

"Remember last month when you dropped the ball?"

"If I do this for you, what will you do for me?"

Or how about this one: "Let me check your performance review and see if you're hitting your numbers. If you are, I may just help you!"

She easily could have asked any of those questions, but she didn't. Instead, in the moment, she acted as a Service Hero by first seeing Jacob as her customer and then, in the spirit of true QBQ Service, choosing to ask a question such as this: "What can I do right now to serve you?" She didn't say, "You succeed, then I'll serve you." Instead she said, "I will work hard to serve you so you can succeed."

QBQ Service is the ultimate win-win situation. "What can I do? How can I serve you today?" The benefits of asking questions such as these are tremendous for everyone involved.

I went back to the Rock Bottom Brewery a couple of months later, looking forward to seeing Jacob again. I felt as if he was my own, personal server. By the way, one of the reasons I remembered his name was that it had such a nice ring to it: Jacob *Miller*. I love his last name!

So I asked the hostess to seat me in Jacob's section, but I was shocked at what she said next: "I'm sorry Sir, Jacob no longer works here."

NO! I thought, You lost my own personal server? You lost a guy who looked at me and thought, What can I do right now to serve you? instead of asking Incorrect Questions such as these:

"Who does the customer think he is, to not read the menu?"

"When are my teammates going to help me out?"

"When is corporate going to provide us the products our customers want?"

"Why are we so busy, busy, busy?"

"Who is supposed to be covering this table, anyway?"

I just couldn't believe they had let him get away!

As I stood in the foyer of the restaurant, all those thoughts were racing through my mind, but I didn't say them. I did finally blurt out, "You've got to be kidding me, you lost him?"

The hostess calmly responded, "We didn't lose him, Sir, we promoted him. He's in Chicago in management."

Of course! We reap what we sow. I had only seen Jacob in action on that one occasion but it only makes sense that the actions I saw and the Service I received were his normal way of doing things. For the Service he gave me, his harvest was the excellent tip I'm sure you would have given him, too. But for what I suspect was a pattern of Personal Accountability and QBQ Service, he was promoted to management.

The Real Rewards

For anyone who has ever worked for tips, there's no question that it feels great to get that bottom-line confirmation of a job well done. But at the same time, a great tip is not going to change your life. For any of us, is the real value in the income? Study after study has shown that pay is not the main motivator for most people. And, although I'm sure Jacob felt good about his promotion, the true reward probably was not the promotion, either.

On the other hand, how do you think Jacob feels about who he is at the end of a day after making accountable choices? No Victim Thinking, no Procrastination, no Blame—just Personal Accountability in action. How do you think he feels about himself when he does *not* ask questions beginning with "Why," "When" or "Who," but asks "What" and "How"? I believe Jacob, his manager and Kristi at L.L. Bean must feel extremely satisfied with the results they get from accountable thoughts and actions, and that is the greatest reward.

When we sow through Service to others, we reap the rewards of feeling more worthy and capable, and more deserving of good things in our lives. Those feelings propel us ever forward, helping us find success and happiness, whatever road we choose to travel.

"Today's My Last Day"

In 1989, I was driving to a prospective client's company for a sales call. I had just bought my first car phone for $950. Hard to believe, isn't it? The air time charges took some getting used to, but I was especially happy to have it that particular day because I was lost. I dialed the company's number and I'll never forget the woman who answered. Her name was Stephanie.

With both joy and warmth in her voice (on a Monday morning, no less), Stephanie asked if I would hold.

"No problem," I said. After about a minute of expensive air time had passed, I was just about to hang up when she came back on and said, "Mr. Miller, are you still there?"

"Yes I am," I said, and then came the words I've never forgotten.

"I'm so thankful you held for me!" Her voice was sincere and positive.

"That's fine," I said. I proceeded to tell her my problem and she gave me directions, but mostly I was thinking about her choice of words. Thankful? She said she was *thankful* I had held for her, and I could tell that she was.

I have to tell you, by acknowledging my patience and thanking me as she did, she made me feel as if I had a 20-inch sign around my neck that said, "I'm special! I'm important!" So when I arrived at her building moments later, I couldn't wait to meet her and I was not disappointed. She was everything I had imagined. Not only did she offer me a gracious welcome, but she was also friendly, upbeat and energetic.

After getting settled into the lobby, I walked to the reception counter, leaned across and spoke quietly. "Stephanie, if this organization's not careful, somebody is going to steal you away!"

She smiled, this person who so enjoys serving others, and said, "Someone already did. Today's my last day!"

Clearly, that company did not see Stephanie as its customer. Don't let that happen to you. Don't let today be the last day for any of the customers in your life. Let it instead be the first day of new relationships built on QBQ Service!

Making Service Personal

Is there someone in your life today with whom your relationship is not as good as it could be? If so, consider going to that person, face to face if possible, and asking these relationship-changing QBQs:

1. "What can I do for you today?"

2. "How can I better meet your expectations?"

3. "What action can I take to help you do your job?"

4. "How can I lighten your burden right now?"

Remember, the answers are in the questions. Don't be surprised if you get some great responses, because the other person just may answer those questions. And then you'll both be well on your way to discovering the powerful difference the Pillar of Service can make in your lives.

Pillar Principle Three: Courage

"Ladies and Gentlemen, for your final exam today, please answer this question in no fewer than one thousand words: 'What is courage?' And do, please, try to make it as coherent and articulate as possible. You have two hours. You may begin."

Several hundred college sophomores went to work, busily thinking and writing. The philosophy professor, assuming none of his students would be finished for at least an hour, was planning to work on some papers from another class. Just as he began, to his surprise, a young woman appeared at his desk, not three minutes into the assignment. She smiled, plopped her booklet on his desk, and quietly left the room.

As the sound of her footsteps disappeared down the hall, he reached for her paper, and there read as good an essay on courage as he'd ever seen.

"What is courage?"

"This is!"

I don't know what he gave her, but I think she deserved an A+. Why? Because she didn't just talk about courage, she took it to the next level and demonstrated it by acting courageously. Sure, she took a risk: His assignment specifically requested "no fewer than one thousand words." But she saw that by stretching beyond the lines he had drawn, she could do a better job of answering the question, so she took the chance. That's courage!

Our third Pillar Principle is Courage and like the others, it stands on its own. But Courage is also closely linked to the other Pillar Principles, because without Courage, it is unlikely we will practice the other Pillars. For example, Courage is required to practice Learning, our first Pillar.

Courage to Learn

I spoke about the QBQ at Traveler's Express and when I was done, a woman made a highly unusual statement: "Well, John, because of you I'm going to go spend $5,500!"

I was thinking, "Oh great, blame me!" But I smiled and inquired, "Whatever do you mean?"

"I'll be 50 next month," she said, "and I've been thinking about going back to school. It will mean some financial hardship and inconvenience for my family, and I have to tell you, I'm scared. It could be tough. But thanks to your message today, I'm going to do it!"

It takes Courage to embrace the Pillar Principle of Learning, but the rewards are great.

The Call of the Comfortable

What can we do to develop Courage? The first thing is to realize what we're up against. One of the main factors that holds us back is the Call of the Comfortable.

People naturally seek comfort. I've heard story after story of people saving up for the trip of a lifetime to some exotic place, excited to experience a new culture, only to get there and stay at the Holiday Inn and eat at McDonald's. We seek the familiar and the comfortable. This is true even in times of crisis.

Sue started her career with Pillsbury in Chicago. She was 22 years of age and new to the Windy City. For the first year or so, she lived in a small apartment outside the heart of downtown, and each day she would ride the bus to and from work.

One evening after working much later than usual, she was sitting on a bench waiting for her bus when a man suddenly approached from the shadows, asking her for the time. There was something unsettling about him, even beyond his scruffy looks. He spoke just above a whisper and his eyes were hidden by the hood of a winter parka, even though it was April.

Sue looked around and seeing no one else for at least half a block, started to feel very nervous. Should I run, she wondered, or answer his question? She chose the latter.

As she lifted her wrist to the light to better see her watch, he lunged for her purse, the strap of which was still wrapped around her arm. Sue reacted quickly and, with her other arm, grabbed the purse and clutched it tightly to her chest.

They struggled for a few moments, she with the purse and he with the strap, locked in a frantic tug-of-war, until, suddenly, out of nowhere, the gleaming blade of a hunting knife flashed in front of Sue's face. Sue, being brave but not foolish, concluded it was time to give up and let go. But then something funny happened.

Her attacker was obviously not a competent crook. Mugging people was probably his avocation rather than his vocation. For some reason known only to him, he cut the strap, which immediately sent him flying backward, falling hard to the ground. Sue took the opportunity to run. A moment later, she boarded a bus carrying her purse and never saw the man again.

At this point in her tale, I said, "Sue, that's some story! What did you do next, go to the police?" I was about to be dumbfounded.

"No John," she said, "I went to Marshall Field's."

"Really? I can't believe you could go shopping after a traumatic experience like that. What were you looking for, a new purse?"

"Oh no. Nothing like that. See, I grew up on a farm in Rockford, Illinois, and once a year, around the holidays, Mom and Dad would pile my six brothers and sisters and me into the station wagon and all nine of us would go into Chicago. It was the highlight of the holiday season."

"OK. So ... ?"

"Well," she continued, "we always spent half the day at Marshall Field's because it was Mom's favorite place. John, I know that place like the back of my hand. I went there that night because I knew that, above any other place, I would feel *comfortable* there."

Returning to the familiar and comfortable is a deep-seated instinct in us all. It's easy to return each day to the "Marshall Field's" of our lives. There's nothing inherently wrong with doing so, of course, but if we're not careful, the desire to be comfortable can turn into a trap that keeps us from growing.

The Call of the Comfortable can be so powerful that it becomes our prison. Andre, a probation officer from Detroit, once told me how the call literally can imprison us.

Every day, he said, he observes the tremendous desire his "customers" have for "hots and cots." He confirmed what I had heard before: As bad as prison life is, inmates get used to three hot meals a day and a cot to sleep on, and some of them would have an incredibly difficult time remaining on the outside. In fact, many of Andre's "customers" had purposely committed a crime just so they could go back to prison, and get back to the comfort of their "hots and cots."

Are you locked in your own prison of the comfortable? Have you become so attached to the way things are that you're unwilling to change to make them better? Denying the Call of the Comfortable is part of developing the Courage to stretch ourselves by taking risks.

The Dangerous Dead Space

The Call of the Comfortable keeps us in what has been called our comfort zones. While this is not a new phrase, it's as relevant as ever. What is a comfort zone? Here's how I describe it:

A defined domain of surroundings and actions in which I experience complete comfort

The comfort zone concept is not unlike the principle of dead space on a thermostat. We all know a thermostat has a range of temperatures in which it does not function. Essentially, it has a dead space of about six degrees. Here's how it works. Let's say you set your control at 68 degrees. When the room temperature rises above 71, the cooling system will kick in and push it back below 71. If the room temperature drops below 65 degrees, the furnace fires up to lift it back to 65 or a little higher.

Here's the key: As long as the temperature remains between 65 and 71 degrees, nothing happens. The dead space prevails.

Each of us has a dead space, that defined domain of surroundings and actions with which we are so completely comfortable we're doing nothing new—certainly not learning, changing and growing.

To simply say, "That's not within my comfort zone," or "That's just the way I am," is not Personal Accountability. Leaders who think and act accountably understand that the objective of practicing the Courage Pillar is to expand the breadth, depth and width of their domains, their comfort zones.

Expansion Requires Risk

Early in my sales career, I was trained to make cold calls by phone to a corporation's president, vice president of sales or sales manager. One day, fresh out of the training program and raring to go with my newly acquired techniques, I got Jonas Mayer of the American Linen Company on the phone.

He sounded old to me, which at the time meant he was over 40. I started into my spiel, leading to the big question, "May I please come see you?"

He was polite but direct. "No!" he said. "And by the way," he continued, "that was the most canned phone script I've ever heard." (Obviously, this was before the rise of modern telemarketing!)

"Gee, thanks for the feedback," I mumbled. We said our good-byes and that was that. I filed away the 4 x 6 index card that contained his information and my notes.

Three months later, the card popped up in my tickler file. I had been trained to persist and I believed that if as a salesperson I didn't turn some people off, I wouldn't turn any on. As I thought about Jonas, I remembered exactly what he'd told me about my phone presentation. Oh well, no pain, no gain! I dialed. He answered.

After I reminded him we had spoken before, I said, "Jonas, how long have you been in sales?"

"More than 30 years." he said gruffly. I figured as much.

"I know you're the vice president of sales now. May I ask, did you begin your career in sales?"

"Yes," he answered, and I could hear his tough facade coming down.

"When you started selling, Jonas, how many sales did you make in your first 30 days?"

"I guess I didn't make any," he responded. "I was pretty green. Why?"

"Well, Jonas, in my first month I didn't make any either, and you're one of them!"

He laughed a hearty laugh and I saw my opening, so I asked again for permission to visit him and this time he said, "Sure, come on over. I'd love to meet you!"

It was a risk but if I hadn't taken it, I'd never have gotten the meeting. What was the risk? Pain. The pain of rejection, the pain of looking like a fool, the pain of failure. That brings me to my definition of Courage.

Courage is acting in spite of the pain

What that really means is each day we must seek *discomfort*. Discomfort is the opposite of comfort and the solution to expanding my comfort zone. It often means consciously asking the QBQ, "How can I today put myself in uncomfortable surroundings and take uncomfortable actions!"

We've all heard the sayings, "Nothing ventured, nothing gained," and "No pain, no gain." They both speak well to the value of experiencing discomfort or pain and taking risks, but neither of them goes far enough.

Think of the risk a bird takes learning to fly, taking that first jump out of the nest. The action literally means life or death. But without that jump, birds would hardly be birds at all. Similarly, if we don't take risks, we will never become the people we're meant to be. Take a risk today.

Face the Fear

The comfort zone is not our only line of defense against taking risks. Another major factor that holds us back is fear. Fear of what? The unknown, mostly—but sometimes, the known.

Few of us have faced the ultimate fear, though. It's what I call "the click."

A friend of mine, Jeff Burton, had a chance to interview his wife Gina's dad, a World War II veteran who was on the front lines in Okinawa. Jeff asked his father-in-law many questions, including this one: "More than 50 years later, what is your most vivid memory?" Gina's dad said simply, "The click."

Jeff look confused. The war vet continued. "At night, lying in our fox holes waiting for dawn to break so we could kill or be killed, there was a deafening silence—until we heard 'the click.' When that sound broke the night's calm, we knew that not far away in another trench, the enemy had pulled the pin from a grenade and at any moment it would land somewhere near us and explode."

Jeff encouraged him to go on. "When we heard the click, the fear welled up within every man and we knew we could either sit still and pray the grenade didn't land in our lap, or we could climb out of the foxhole and run. If we ran, of course, the enemy would take us with a spray of machine gun fire. Those moments between the click and the explosion were pure hell."

In comparison, do you and I really even know fear? Can we ever understand true Courage when we've never been on the literal front lines? I don't mean to minimize the risks we do take each day, but I wonder if I'd been shot at in a real war with real bullets whether I would have more Courage today.

I ask you to consider the concept of the click. What triggers in you the most bone-chilling fear?

If we want to achieve more in life, at some point we have to face the click.

Release the Past

I went to school one day with my son, Michael, who was eight at the time, to help him with his show-and-tell exhibit. Afterward, we were walking down the hallway when a woman approached us and shrieked, "It's a snake!"

"Ah, yes Ma'am," I said. "It's my son's rosy boa—small, tame and safe."

Michael's brown-and-tan-striped pet snake, Leo, was resting peacefully on Michael's arm. The woman looked at the snake, and again at Michael and said, uncertainly this time, "May I touch it?"

"Sure!" he said as he gently pushed Leo under her nose. She flinched and slowly stretched her hand out toward the creature, then abruptly pulled it back, yelling, "Oh, I can't!"

We assured her she didn't have to touch the snake, though I secretly hoped she would. I would love to see people get past their misconceptions about snakes. They aren't slimy and are more scared of you than you are of them.

She wasn't giving up. She tried to grab Leo's 18-inch-long body but was stopped short, as if by some invisible force, her fingers frozen in space. "Oh, I really can't!" she said again.

At this point I was thinking, Yes, you can, if you choose to. The look on Michael's face was saying, Why doesn't this lady just grab him so we can go home?

Finally, this thirty-something woman named Patti took one index finger and tentatively stroked the snake's back, down to the end of his sleek, smooth, dry body and back up to the neck, freezing purposely just before the head.

"May I hold him?" she asked. "Go ahead," Mike said. Patti took Leo into her hands and something wonderful happened. I saw years of fear disappear, melting away as she experienced one of the most interesting creatures ever created. A visible wave of relief came over her, as if she'd just lain down some great burden. It turns out she had.

When she was age 12, she told us, her parents took her and her older sister on a camping trip to New Mexico. They were to stay in a cabin somewhere between the desert and the mountains. They arrived late at night, only to discover the cabin lights weren't working. So they fumbled around in the dark until they found their bunks. By then, they were so tired, they just fell into bed. They'd deal with the electrical problem in the morning.

Less than five minutes after getting settled in, Patti's mom spoke from the darkness in a forced whisper, "I don't think we're alone in here." Her husband responded, "What are you talking about? It's just the four of us." Ignoring him, she repeated, more urgently this time, "I don't think we're alone in here!"

She slipped from her lower bunk and found her flashlight. Returning to her bed, she gingerly pulled the mattress back, exposing the solid wooden frame underneath. It was then she met the steely eyes and heard the unmistakable rattle of their "guest."

There in the beam of Mom's flashlight, they saw the full form of a six-foot-long timberback rattlesnake, all coiled up, ready to defend its territory. It was poised for the strike and they knew it.

"Needless to say," Patti told us, "no conversation was necessary." There was simply a mad scramble in the darkness and approximately 17 seconds later they found themselves, all four of them, crammed into the front seat of their six-seat sedan.

A quarter-century later, standing in the hallway with Mike and me, Patti exclaimed, "It's a snake!" but somehow found a way to face her fear and set herself free.

Is there something you have been avoiding out of fear, either of the known or unknown? Practicing Personal Accountability means facing that fear. Daring to "touch" it. The object of your fear is rarely as bad as you imagine it, and facing it will help you develop the Courage to overcome it.

QBQ Courage

The QBQ, a method of leadership thinking that enables us to practice Personal Accountability, can help us develop Courage. How? By asking good questions, of course. Here are a few to consider:

"What can I do to avoid the Call of the Comfortable?"

"How can I experience discomfort today?"

"What action (risk) can I take today to expand my comfort zone?"

The answers are in the questions. When you consider these questions, you'll come up with your own answers and ideas. Here are a few that come to mind for me.

1. Acquire new skills.

Without the appropriate skills I cannot move beyond my comfort zone, as much as I desire to do so. Say, for example, I'm a logger working in the forest and you're my manager. Every day I'm working hard, chopping down trees with my trusty, double-bladed axe, which I keep sharp enough to split a hair. You come out to see me for my quarterly performance review and inform me that, though I just finished a record year, I need to produce at a rate of 20 percent above last year. In other words, corporate is "raising the bar."

I'm amazed at your demand and stare at you as if either I didn't hear you correctly or you're one limb short of a tree. "But Boss," I cry, "I'm working 12 hours a day now! I only take a break to sharpen my axe and I always skip lunch. How in the world can I produce more?"

As I'm whining, you get up and walk away, leaving me thinking, "Uh oh. I said too much!" But you return with a brand new, shiny chain saw, well oiled, gassed up and ready to go.

"For me?" I ask, hopefully.

"She's all yours! Isn't she a beaut?"

"Terrific, Boss! Thanks! And oh, by the way, you wanted 20 percent? I can give you 30!"

A new tool—and that's what a new skill is—gives us additional capabilities and new personal confidence, and with those comes the Courage to try. So take a look at where you need to expand your comfort zone, and work on developing some new skills.

2. Change your perspective.

In addition to acquiring new skills, it helps to get a fresh perspective and come at problems from a new direction. I came across a good example of this with three Miller women and the balance beam.

The general idea of the balance beam competition in gymnastics is to do flips, cartwheels and all sorts of other impossible-looking gymnastic feats without falling off.

However, a piece of wood four inches wide by 16 feet long and suspended four feet in the air is not designed to help people stay on—in fact, it's designed to make staying on extremely difficult. Yet according to the rules of the sport, falling off is a bad thing.

But I've learned from three Miller women—my daughter Kristin Miller, who retired from the sport at 13; my older sister, Lucy Miller, who was quite the gymnast in the early '70s; and of course, Shannon Miller (no relation), winner of the 1996 Gold Medal on the balance beam—that there's a better way to view the balance beam. And that is this: Falling off is a good thing!

It's true. A sports psychologist would say that those who achieve in the sport think differently from those who struggle. The high achievers approach the beam each day thinking, "Falling off is good. Let's do some more of that today!"

You see, if a six-year-old girl who's just starting out approaches the balance beam thinking, "I mustn't fall off," chances are she'll either never get on in the first place or if she does, she'll play it too safe ever to become a champion.

But if she has the perspective, "Falling off is good," or at least that falling off is OK in the service of getting better, she'll have the Courage to continue and excel.

How many times do you suppose Shannon Miller has fallen off the balance beam in her lifetime? I'm sure it's too many to count. Why would she do that? Because at some point early on, she came to understand that not only was it *OK* to fall off, but also that falling off was the only way to learn how to do all the amazing feats and stay *on!* So up she went and down she fell, over and over and over again until at the age of 18, she became an Olympic champion and brought home the gold!

Many of us view life as something from which we must not fall. Yet, without the willingness and the desire to fall off some days, how will we ever reach new heights and bring home the gold?

There's an adage that says, "There are no failures if there are lessons learned." My observations of gymnastics and experiences in life prove this true.

As you look at some of the challenges you face in your life, get a new perspective on them. Only then will you find the Courage to fall off enough times to become a champion!

3. Develop resilience.

Bouncing back is a consistent characteristic of all champions. A healthy resilience can enable us to bounce back, even from the worst circumstances.

Most people are familiar with the story of John Thompson, the young man from North Dakota who, after having both arms tragically severed from his body in a farm accident in January 1992, opened the door to his house with his teeth, picked up a pencil in his mouth and dialed 911. Then, to protect the household furnishings from the bloody mess, he climbed into the bathtub to wait for the ambulance. It's an amazing and heroic story.

But I like to share, as Paul Harvey says, "the rest of the story." John was transferred to North Memorial Hospital in Robbinsdale, Minnesota, where the chaplain, Greg Bodin, is a friend of mine. Greg was one of the very first to counsel John after the accident. A year or more later, I asked Greg what, in his opinion, was the most memorable aspect of John's character.

I thought he'd use words such as Courage, belief or confidence, but instead, recalling John fondly, he said, "He had a *resiliency* that I'd never seen before nor have I seen since. He just had an uncanny ability to bounce back."

Have you ever had a bad day? Ever had a month of them? Me too. Still, I know the sum total of all the bad days I've ever had is nothing compared with what that young man faced and still faces.

If you're struggling with taking a risk, know that even in the worst-case scenario, chances are you'll be all right. You can bounce back. And let that knowledge help you find the Courage you need.

4. Take action.

It's *not* the thought that counts. Courage requires action.

I was about to check in for a flight back home to Denver when I overheard a woman in front of me pleading with the gate agent, "You've got to have a seat for me. If I don't catch this flight I'll miss my connection to Rapid City. Then I'll have to drive all night through Nebraska. Are you sure there's no room?"

They told her she could get on the waiting list but it didn't look good, and I watched her walk away with her head hanging low. I wondered to myself if I could help her out by taking a later flight to Denver. But to tell you the truth, the thought passed quickly. It was Sunday evening and I'd been away for four days, 17 hours, and 23 minutes. But who was counting? My family, that's who! And I was, too. I saw all their faces in my mind and decided I didn't want to arrive home at midnight when I could be home for dinner.

I walked over to the young woman, not to give her my seat but to offer encouragement. "I hope you get on," I said.

"Thanks, I'm trying to get home for my parents' 30th wedding anniversary." Ouch! Did she have to tell me that?

Probably trying to relieve my own conscience more than anything else, I told her I had thought about giving her my seat but had a family waiting at home.

She responded appropriately by smiling and saying, "Oh, how nice of you!"

Right then, a man who'd obviously been listening to our conversation stepped up and said, "Young lady, 'nice' would be doin' it, not thinkin' it!"

I agreed and we all had a good laugh. The man was right: it's not the thinkin', it's the doin'. Courageous thoughts don't make the difference, only courageous actions do.

Making Courage Personal

Every day, courageous people are taking actions such as these:

• Making a tough cold call on a new prospect
• Confronting an employee who's off track
• Asking the difficult question of the buying customer
• Leveling with the boss about a problem
• Starting a new business
• Admitting "I was wrong"
• Quitting a salaried position to go back to school

Simply put, they're facing their fears and taking the risks necessary to accomplish their goals and do what they believe is right.

To take similar risks, we must watch out for the Call of the Comfortable and ask QBQs every day such as, "What can I do today to be more courageous?" Then we can all experience the difference the Pillar of Courage makes!

Take a moment to write out your answers to these questions:

1. In what areas of my life do I need more Courage?

2. Since we all have things we've been "thinkin'" but not "doin'," what are some of those things in my work life? My home life?

3. How will I face my fear and expand my comfort zone?

4. By practicing the Pillar Principle of Courage, how will I and those around me gain?

5. What specific courageous action will I take today?

Pillar Principle Four: Excellence

When I was at Cornell in the late '70s, there was a football player named Bobby who was a third-string quarterback and part-time kicker. In his four years, he had never actually played the quarterback position.

Near the end of the season, in the quest for the Ivy League championship, Cornell was in a crucial game against Yale. Cornell was favored to win but its first-string quarterback got hurt in the first quarter. From then on it was a very close, hard-fought game.

With two minutes to go and only a three-point lead, Cornell's second-string quarterback went down with a knee injury, and everyone in the stadium knew what that meant: Only Bobby was left. The coach turned to Bobby and used these motivational words, "Well, Son, I guess we're gonna *have* to put you in."

Now *there's* a coach!

Bobby leaped from the bench, "Yes Sir, Coach, what should I do?" he asked, excited for his first chance to play.

"Bobby, we're up 6-3, so here's exactly what I want you to do. On the first play, tuck that ball away real tight so you don't drop it, then put your head down and run to the right. On the second play, do the same thing but run to the left. On the third play, run right up the center. OK? Now this is very important, Bobby, so listen closely to me now. I know you can kick, so that's what I want you to do. On the fourth play, I want you to take that ball and punt it as high and far as you possibly can! You got all that?"

"Yes Sir, Coach!" Bobby said, and ran onto the field, eager to do exactly what the coach had told him. Starting on his own 10-yard line on the first play, he clutched the ball as if his life depended on it and ran to the right. To everyone's surprise, he ran 17 yards! The crowd cheered. On the second play he ran to the left and got 21 more yards. Unbelievable! He'd taken the team halfway down the field in a matter of seconds.

The crowd was on its feet. On the third play, running right up the center, Bobby broke through all the tackles except one, and was stopped just six inches short of the goal line. The crowd was going wild! A touchdown would virtually guarantee a win and the championship. In the huddle though, Bobby remembered the coach's instructions.

As the team set up for the fourth play, the crowd quickly quieted down, not believing what it was seeing. Bobby lined up to punt, and with six inches to go for a touchdown, did exactly what he was told: He kicked the ball as far and high as he possibly could, sending it clear out of the stadium. It bounced in the parking lot.

The crowd was in shock and the coach was furious. Unable to control himself, he ran on to the field, shook Bobby by the shoulder pads and screamed, "You stupid idiot, what could you possibly have been thinking when you kicked that pigskin?"

Bobby, always the respectful young man, replied, "Well, Sir, I was thinking I must have just about the *dumbest coach in all of football!*"

Do you believe that story? Did you enjoy it anyway? Good. I enjoy sharing it because of what it so vividly illustrates.

Let's push instant replay and take a closer look. First, the coach told Bobby what to do: In corporate terms, he might have said, "We need 20 percent more!" Bobby, like most of us, was eager to perform and collect the rewards. What would have helped him do so was an excellent coach.

When Bobby didn't score, even though he did follow the coach's instructions, who did the coach blame? Bobby. Instead of asking the QBQ, "How can I be a more effective coach for you?" he pointed his finger at Bobby and asked an IQ, "Why didn't you … ?"

This bully-and-blame style will never lead to Excellence. You can't *make* people achieve Excellence, no matter how hard you try, and nobody can force you to be excellent. As individuals, though, each of us can decide to pursue our fourth Pillar Principle, Excellence. And the key to Excellence is effective coaching.

If you want to help others achieve Excellence, set your sights on being an excellent coach. If you want Excellence in yourself, set your sights on getting a coach. Yes, that's what I said. Regardless of who we are, what we do or what we already have achieved, you and I can gain tremendously from having a coach. But first, let's explore the Pillar Principle itself.

What is Excellence?

Excellence means different things to different people:

• Being the best of the best
• Raising the bar
• Overcoming the obstacles
• Owning the market
• Setting—and achieving—new standards
• Being Number One

Here's how I define Excellence:

Celebrating the achievement of a new level of performance while setting my sights beyond

Excellence, to me, is an attitude, a mindset, a desire for continuous improvement. What kills our ability to achieve Excellence? Simple. These IQs and others like them:

"Why don't people just accept me the way I am?"
"When will I get the recognition I deserve?"
"Who said I need to improve?"

This last IQ clearly denotes defensiveness. I recall that as a teen, my dad always taught me to drive defensively on the road. Driving defensively, watching the other cars at all times, is a good thing. But *living* defensively is a bad thing. When we defend ourselves, we're not practicing Personal Accountability, are we? Our ability to achieve Excellence dies quickly with a defensive posture.

Practicing the Pillar Principle of Excellence means asking two sets of QBQs:

"What actions can I take to lift myself to the next level?" and "How can I elevate my performance?"

plus,

"How can I appreciate where I am?" and "What can I do right now to celebrate my recent achievements?"

The first set of questions enables us to continue the growth process. The second set gives us permission to appreciate where we are.

How can we achieve Excellence? From my own personal life and my observations of peak performers in organizations across many industries, I've concluded that people rarely achieve Excellence without outside help—in other words, effective coaching. It's an undisputed fact that athletic teams need good coaches to guide them in mastering certain skills while continuing to hone their natural abilities. In the same way, individuals and teams can gain tremendously from the direction of a competent and committed coach.

Coaching has been a popular topic in business books over the past couple of decades. I won't try to provide a comprehensive description of an effective coach here, but there are some essential coaching skills we can apply to all kinds of relationships—managing, supporting a team member, encouraging a friend and parenting, to name a few. We also can seek out coaches for ourselves with these abilities. Here are seven I've found helpful. Excellent coaches ...

1. Paint verbal pictures.

Picture yourself in a prison cell. All the guards have gone to sleep. From two cells away, another prisoner whispers to you that he has the key to your cell. The problem is, there's absolutely no way he physically can get it to you. His cell is around the corner. He can't throw, bounce, slide or bank-shot it to your cell. I ask you, of what value to you is this tool, the key? Zip!

When you pictured this scenario in your mind, didn't the image communicate the idea? When a coach possesses an idea that can help me grow, I will only gain if he or she can communicate it to me in such a way that I can comprehend it, believe it and apply it.

My speaking coach, David Levin, is an excellent example of this principle. One of the first things he talked about with me was the importance of making a strong "connection" with the audience.

The idea that I must connect with the audience before I could have an impact on them wasn't necessarily new. But David was able to help me see how some little things I was saying and doing were having a negative impact on that connection. There was a link between the concept and the practice that I hadn't seen or understood before. He painted the picture so I could understand.

When I started removing those "separators," as we call them, from my talks, there was a marked difference. I immediately could feel the improved connection with and impact on the audience. David's ability to take an abstract concept such as connection and translate it into clear, practical terms made all the difference for me.

A good coach is a good communicator. Since the mind does not think in words, but in pictures, an effective coach paints the picture to ensure communication of the idea. Learn to use metaphors, analogies and stories to paint those verbal pictures.

2. Admit mistakes.

I started my first job out of college in 1980, at Cargill Inc., as a commodities trader (corn, soybeans, wheat, oats). My daily purpose was to "buy low, sell high." While still at Cornell and in the process of interviewing with Cargill, I asked Cargill's recruiter what sort of performance would be expected of me. I was a bit apprehensive, but to my relief he said, "It's our hope that you'll be right on a trade 51 times out of 100."

No one is right about everything. When we pretend we are, we break down trust. When we're wrong about something, it's healthy to admit it. Coaching is usually a two-way street anyway, with each party learning from the other. If I can't approach coaching from either side with a humble spirit, admitting when I'm wrong, I'll never develop the trust and communication necessary to achieve Excellence. The best coaches understand this truth: *Humility is the cornerstone of leadership.*

3. Create an encouraging environment.

Many years ago, I called on Richard, then the vice president of sales at a software firm, manager of about a dozen salespeople. Richard had an archaic belief that sales managers could and should motivate their people through threats, fear and manipulation. "By any means necessary," was his rule. Thoughts and emotions based on this belief drove his management practices, particularly when his salespeople failed to make their goals.

One of Richard's practices was something I hope your coach never does to you, nor you or I ever do to another. Based on the IQ, "Why aren't my people motivated?" rather than the QBQ, "What can I do to be a more effective leader?" he bought a 50-gallon fish tank and put it in his office. He got a dozen tropical fish of various kinds, and assigned one to each salesperson.

Then he divided the tank in half. He placed the tropical fish on one side. On the other, he put in a piranha, a big one! Can you see it coming? At the end of every 30 days, he would call the whole sales force into his corner office and announce the identity of the lowest performer for that month. Then he would scoop out the corresponding fish, and all 13 people in the room would ceremoniously watch the piranha devour that month's "loser." Can you imagine?

If there's anything good about that story, it is that even people with beliefs such as these can come to see the error of their ways.

I met up with Richard a decade later. He's back with the same company now after working for another firm for a few years. The tank in his office is long gone. As he puts it, "I've grown up."

"John," he said, "I don't do fish any more. I've changed."

"How have you changed?" I asked.

"I've shifted my view on how to motivate salespeople. In fact, I've come to understand that I can't motivate them. They must motivate themselves!"

Richard finally understood: Motivation from within propels all of us to the next level of Excellence. One person cannot motivate another. Either we have that spark, that desire to achieve, or we don't.

If we can't make people achieve, then what *can* we do? The coach can work toward creating the right environment to allow natural motivation and the drive for success to come to the surface.

In looking at my life and the lives of so many others, I've come to believe that the foundation of Excellence is not only in the "want to" of people, but in the environment around them. The coach is the key to building the right environment for Excellence.

When I was age 35, I decided to look for a specific kind of coach: a guitar teacher. I went out and bought myself a brand new blue guitar (yes, blue). While at the store, I asked the manager if he knew a good teacher, and he recommended Ellie Borkon of Golden Valley, Minnesota.

At the first lesson, Ellie sat this successful salesperson, loving husband and fantastic father of four (a legend in his own mind!) on a stool and asked him to sing. I have confidence in a lot of my abilities, but my singing isn't one of them. Nevertheless, Ellie encouraged me to sing anything I wished. "Whenever you're ready," she urged gently. "I just want to hear how you sound." It wasn't long before I found myself in front of someone I had just met, singing.

In this vulnerable position, any hint of ridicule or sarcasm certainly would have embarrassed me. I doubt I would've come back. Ellie continued to encourage me, though. She gave me Courage to sing out loud. She nodded her head and smiled, letting me know she understood this was risky for me.

Some months later, I talked to her about this experience and how grateful I was for her kindness toward me. "Everyone can sing," she asserted. "They just have to find the right key for their voice." She saw her role as helping to provide the right key, the right environment, for her students to perform to their best ability.

Ellie was an excellent coach, though I doubt she knew it. She understood intuitively the best way to change human behavior. She was always positive, but not in a false way. She commented on my strengths and didn't mention my flaws, which were many. Her enthusiasm and encouragement built my confidence, enabling me to learn and to grow more sure of myself without the fear of failure. Her intent was always to help me, and I never felt "beat up."

Ellie was a natural at creating the proper environment for Excellence. Most of us are not, but we can learn by applying these ideas.

4. Exist to serve.

Effective coaches do what effective leaders do: They exist to serve others. They are there for the right reasons. Their purpose is to have those around them become Number One by achieving Excellence, rather than becoming Number One themselves. They really care about whether you succeed. Good coaches are there to counsel, not change; help, not hurt; encourage, not embarrass. To have the greatest positive impact, a coach must have the right intentions.

If I'm doing the coaching, I need to check my own heart. Is it in the right place? Am I more excited about what someone else can become than what the relationship will do for me? If not, I may want to reconsider my role, or work on my own thinking by asking the QBQs, "How can I help another reach her goals through Excellence?" and "What can I do to celebrate his successes with him?"

If you're looking for a coach, to a certain extent, you have to trust your instincts. Coaching relationships are very complex and there will always be complicating factors such as position, status, relationship, money and power. But the bottom line is that a good coach will be committed to helping you achieve Excellence, and if his or her heart is in the right place, you'll be able to feel it, as I could with Ellie. Everything she did communicated that she was there only to serve by helping me accomplish my goals.

5. Celebrate each success.

In my work with corporations, I've heard a lot of talk about "raising the bar," which may sound like an attitude of Excellence. Unfortunately, it's more likely just Corporate saying, "OK, last year's numbers are worth about as much as yesterday's newspaper. Now we need 20 percent more!"

The main problem with this approach is that there's no celebration. And the road to Excellence should be paved with great celebration!

Ask yourself: Do I celebrate? How about my organization? Or is there always a push to accomplish more, more, more? When people resist the word celebration, I have to wonder about their organizational culture. Where there is little celebration, often there is an underlying, collective struggle with perfectionism. Where perfectionism is present, few achievements can meet the high standards required for celebration.

The paradox is that where there is little celebration, there is little Excellence. Celebration is more than the reward we receive for having just arrived at our current level. It's also the fuel that lifts us to the next level. Let's look again at our definition of the Pillar Principle of Excellence:

Celebrating the achievement of a new level of performance while setting my sights beyond

Perhaps for you, as for me, the word celebration carries with it an image of party hats and streamers. Though that can be a valid picture, it's not what I have in mind. Celebration takes place when a leader lets her team know how proud she is of its most recent triumphs. She may celebrate through a kind word, a note, an unexpected call or a lunch out. Or celebration may mean blowing an old bugle that hangs on the wall of the office each time a sale is made.

You may feel celebrated when a plant from the florist arrives unexpectedly at your front door. That's how my manager, Jim Strutton, celebrated my success one time. I was home alone working in my basement office when the doorbell rang. I was on the phone, and went to the door several minutes later to find nobody there. But on the step was a five-foot-tall house tree—not for me, but for my wife.

Jim was letting her know how glad he was to have both of us "on the team" and how proud of me he was for that month's sales performance. It was, at least for John and Karen Miller, the perfect thing to do at that time. The only problem was that the florist had left a bright red tag hanging from an upper leaf. It said, "Reduced - 50% off"! Oh well, it's the thought that ... .

Celebration is anything that says, "Yes, you (or we) did it." and "Wow, aren't you special!" I once heard it said that happiness is "enjoying the moment." Happiness also can be enjoying the process of growth. We can work to progress to higher levels of achievement while still reveling in life right here, right now. We do that simply by celebrating our arrival at each new level.

6. Know what to say when.

It was 1976. I was a senior and the captain of the Ithaca High School wrestling team. My father, Jimmy Miller, was "Mr. Wrestling" in Ithaca, New York. He had been the Cornell University wrestling coach for more than 25 years and the team had won the Ivy League championship title most of the years he coached. As an individual grappler himself in the '40s, he had won the Eastern Intercollegiate Tournament against young men from Navy, Penn State, Army and Lehigh—the powerhouses of the East. He took home the National AAU's top award twice. And in 1948 he missed making the Olympic team by one match. (Believe me, I've heard the story!) So Jimmy Miller's son was expected to win.

One winter evening, I was on the mat for a six-minute match and doing great. But why shouldn't I have been? My opponent was only a sophomore from Cortland, New York. I should defeat a boy two years behind me from a small school, I thought.

My advantage came quickly as I took him to the ground, scoring extra points for exposing his back to the mat. The first two-minute period went fast and I found myself up nine points to zero. I was having fun and so were the 500 parents in the Ithaca High gymnasium—especially Mr. Wrestling himself.

At the start of the second period, the referee gave me the choice of taking the "down" position on my hands and knees underneath my adversary, or taking the upper position, on top of my opponent. Thanks to my confidence and the belief that I could escape from him easily, I chose the bottom position.

The whistle blew. I bolted to a standing position, the Cortland wrestler behind me with arms locked around my waist. I worked on breaking his grip and turned to face him, but I turned too soon. His hands weren't parted yet. We were face to face but he had the bear-hug advantage and I had nothing, including my balance. The heel of my right foot caught on the inside of my left ankle and I fell backward as he landed squarely on top of me! It happened fast and yet seemed to take place in slow motion. The referee was merciful. He quickly slapped the mat and it was over.

My 15-year-old opponent danced around the mat in excitement. Who could blame him? He'd just pinned the twelfth-grade captain of the Ithaca High team at home before a stunned crowd. How do you think I felt in that moment? I was heartsick. Devastated.

In spite of my performance, our team won easily. Afterward, since we were the home team, our job was to roll up the mats and put them away, and my dad waited patiently to drive me home. Looking back now as a parent myself, I wonder how great his hurt was for me. I think I know.

As we were about to leave the gym, Shari, a girl a year behind me in school, approached excitedly with that night's program and a pen in hand. She asked if I would give her my "autograph". I did, somewhat reluctantly. Why would she want a loser to sign his name? My dad, the coach, witnessed it all.

Then Shari and my teammates were gone. It was only Dad and me. With perfect timing he said something that is still imprinted on my mind today: "You know, Johnny, that gal sees you as a hero tonight *simply because you're you.*"

With those well-timed words, he helped me lift myself up when I was down.

The coaches who make a difference "pick their battles." They don't tear you down when you're already as low as a snake's belly, saying things that destroy your confidence and sense of self. They pick their words and moments with care. Instead of being flippant, they make positive, purposeful comments. There's no spirit of meanness, only meaningfulness.

Jerry Twentier from Texas, a nice guy and the author of *The Positive Power of Praising People,* demonstrates throughout his book the importance of lifting people up with the words we use. Good coaches do that constantly. They know what to say and when to say it. Are they perfect? No. Do they have good timing? Yes, they do. And this timing is essential to good coaching.

7. Draw people out.

In 1986, Jim Strutton, who sent Karen and me the tree for our home, hired me to sell training for Steve Brown's company, The Fortune Group. One of Jim's primary purposes was to go on sales calls with me so he could observe my progress and help me grow. It was always fun to have Jim come along because his intent was crystal clear: to enable me to achieve Excellence. As my coach, Jim always practiced Personal Accountability. He never asked IQs such as, "Why didn't you make the sale?" or "When are you going to start producing?"

He'd use the QBQ, "How can I help John achieve his goals?"

Not every call went as planned, though.

Together we called on a company called Business Incentives, now BI Performance Services. Al Prentice, an easy-going man who was vice president of marketing, was my primary contact. I had called on Al to offer him our sales management training program, and our one-on-one visit went well. Later he told me he liked the materials I showed him, my youthful enthusiasm and my focus on making the sale. But what I didn't know, because I didn't ask, was that he happened to be looking for a training program to use for BI's sales managers, and so I had come along at a particularly opportune time. We agreed to meet again.

I returned, along with Jim Strutton, to make my presentation to the senior vice president and four area vice presidents of the corporation. This was the biggest sales call I had made up to that point, and I was well prepared with sales material, videos, books and memorized answers to every potential objection.

What I didn't count on was Roger. Roger was an area vice president who happily took the role of devil's advocate. When I made a point he would ask, "So how are you any different from Wilson Learning?" When I suggested a difference, he would respond, "That doesn't mean your program would work better here than theirs would, does it?"

I back-pedaled and he threw me another zinger, "Why shouldn't we just send our managers to the Dale Carnegie program?" And the meeting went downhill from there. Jim Strutton watched from the back of BI's executive boardroom, never saying a word. Needless to say, I didn't make the sale.

When Jim and I left BI's building, we got into the car and, to my surprise, the first thing he did was tell me about two things I did well, how great he felt about them and how pleased he was with my progress. Then he engaged in the Number One skill of coaching: questioning. He drew me out. He got me thinking about the call, the process, the people, the tactics I used and Roger's comments.

Essentially, he had me visualizing how the call went and how to do it better next time. The question he repeatedly asked was this: "John, if you had it do to over again, what would you do differently?" I told him, but in reality I was telling myself. All learning is self-discovery and Jim Strutton knew that well.

Too many of us see ourselves as Great Problem Solvers. I discovered this through the content of The Fortune Group's programs. But the perspective of outstanding coaches is really the 180-degree opposite. In business or at home, effective coaches are Problem *Givers*. They turn people's challenges into growth opportunities. When someone comes to them with an issue, challenge, dilemma or problem, they don't provide the answer. They help others find it for themselves.

In my role as a parent, as a business consultant or as a friend, I need to be a Problem Giver, not a Problem Solver. I want to be the kind of coach who challenges others to use their creativity to solve their own problems. Socrates used questions to teach. He knew the answer was within the "student," and he just needed to bring it out. The Socratic questioning technique is the best way to return the problem that requires solving back to the person who presented it.

Here's a technique I recommend for developing the skill of drawing others out. It's simple, practical and easy to remember—and it works. I call it The Seven Magic Words of Leadership:

"I don't know. What do you think?"

Count 'em, there are seven. Next time one of your teammates, associates or children approaches you with a question or a problem, don't give an answer. Don't play the role of omniscient Problem Solver. Turn the question/problem back to the other person and allow him or her to solve the problem. Ask, "I don't know, What do you think?"

This doesn't mean you don't care. It just means that you understand, as Socrates did, that a well-placed question is one of the best tools you can use to help others attain Excellence. In fact, if a coach could only possess one skill, one arrow in the quiver, I believe it should be the skill of drawing people out through questions.

The Power of Personal Coaching

We've identified seven abilities of excellent coaches. They ...

1. Paint verbal pictures.
2. Admit mistakes.
3. Create an encouraging environment.
4. Exist to serve.
5. Celebrate each success.
6. Know what to say when.
7. Draw people out.

But I want to make this very clear: if you are committed to your own Excellence, you must get yourself a coach! In my opinion, nobody can truly excel without coaching.

Excellence in sports always involves coaching. Try to imagine a championship team or an individual Olympic champion going for the gold without a coach. It just doesn't happen.

The same thing is true inside our organizations. Excellent individuals and teams have excellent managers-leaders-coaches. But if managers, leaders and coaches want to be excellent, they need coaching too. Whether you're in an official or informal leadership role, you simply can't afford to ignore the power of having a coach.

"Not me!"

I wouldn't be surprised if you were resisting this idea right now. I know I did! In 1995 I attended my first National Speakers Association convention, held in Minneapolis. Harvey Mackay, the CEO of Mackay Envelope and author of the best seller *Swim with the Sharks,* was one of the heavy-duty speakers on the program.

As I listened to him with my arms crossed and my jaw tight—because I was thinking I should be up there on the platform—he said, "Every professional speaker needs a coach!" and I instantly rejected the idea.

Not me! I thought. I've sold training and I've been in front of groups for nine years. I don't need a coach. I'm different.

Do you recognize that mindset from the Pillar of Learning? It's the Exception Excuse: "This sounds good, but it certainly doesn't apply to me!" The Exception Excuse is a Roadblock to Learning that also can be a major barrier to striving for Excellence.

Don't let this Roadblock stop you.

I hesitate to tell this next story for fear it will sound as if I'm boasting about myself. That is not the purpose at all. I share this only to show how I came to understand that I needed a coach.

One night in early 1997 I gave a talk that I thought went particularly well. I was speaking for the Peak Performers Network in Minneapolis to a group of about 1,500 people—an accomplishment in itself, I felt. I was opening up for Lou Holtz, the famous former Notre Dame football coach. I don't mind telling you that I was nervous, but at the same time, I'd worked hard to be there and was proud to be on the same platform with him.

The talk did go well—so well, in fact, that when I finished, the audience stood as they applauded. It was quite a thrill!

In business, there are certain measurements you look at to gauge your progress and success: sales, customer satisfaction, productivity, net profit and so forth.

As a speaker, I also have ways to assess how I'm doing. A few of these are feedback from the people who hire me, which turns up in good referrals and repeat business; the general trend in my business, that is, the growth of annual revenue and fees per engagement; and of course, the response from the audience.

By every objective and subjective measurement I could make, things were going well. And especially on that night, what else could I have thought except, "Hey, this is great! Things are really kicking into gear now. I have arrived."

But David Levin was in the audience that night. He wasn't officially coaching me yet but we had known each other for a while and were starting to become friends, so I had invited him to share my "big night" with me.

The next day I called him, flush with feelings of success from the night before, excited to talk about it. It was during that phone call that he first suggested perhaps I could benefit from some coaching. That was a hard pill to swallow, especially right after my "moment of glory," but we had a solid foundation of trust, so I heard him out. It wasn't that he thought I had done poorly—he was as pleased as I was with the response—it's just that he was more excited by the vision he had for how much better I could become.

Do you hear the difference? That's what the Pillar of Excellence is all about, and I hate to think how different things would be for me today if I had let my feeling of having arrived keep me from listening to David that day. The IQ, "Who said I need to improve?" would have been devastating not only to my career, but to my ability to help people with the message of Personal Accountability. Don't let that happen to you.

Why We All Need Coaches

Even if we're good at coaching others, we still need coaching for ourselves. Editors who write need editors for their own work. Actors who direct still need directors when they're acting. Player-coaches certainly need coaches when they play.

Regardless of who we are or what we do, you and I can gain tremendously from having a coach. Here are just three reasons we need a coach to keep us on the road of Excellence.

1. Coaches help us slay the demon of complacency.

There's a close cousin to the Exception Mentality that creeps into our lives and keeps us from Excellence. I've heard it described as a demon that stalks us daily. It has an eight-foot wing span, a gargoyle-like head, razor-sharp talons and a knife-like beak. This demon drifts slowly into our lives and enters our very being. If it remains undetected, eventually it will inhabit the depths of our souls. It is the demon of complacency. All right, maybe this is a little melodramatic, but it makes the point: Complacency is a major problem.

The definition of complacency:

A feeling of self-satisfaction wrapped in a dangerous unawareness of my own personal deficiencies

When complacency settles in, we can become blinded to the reality around us, as if in a trance. All is well, we think to ourselves.

The danger is that this mentality leads to stagnation, which means we are not advancing or developing. While we sit and pat ourselves on our backs about our recent successes, the world passes us by. I've heard it said that business is like a shark that needs to keep moving to breathe. If it stops moving, it dies. Nothing is ever static. We are either progressing or regressing. People are like that too. Complacency is a killer.

When I've achieved a new level of success, the coaches in my life have helped me overcome complacency by encouraging me to take my focus off how well things are going—once I've had a chance to celebrate a recent achievement, of course. They've helped me avoid congratulating myself about how much I already know and instead set my sights on the next level, which is what Excellence is all about.

Identify a coach in your life and enlist him or her to help you slay the demon of complacency.

2. Coaches enable us to climb the ladder of learning.

A coach enables us to progress up the four rungs on the Ladder of Learning:

Awareness. Have you ever had a "V8" experience? I'm not referring to a V8 car engine, but to the old television commercials for the vegetable drink, in which, right after drinking a can of soda, the person dramatically slapped her forehead as she suddenly realized, "Wow! I could have had a V8!" That's awareness. We experience it when our eyes have been opened, when we've broken through denial. Coaches lead us to a greater awareness of our own strengths and weaknesses. With this awareness, we can use the resources at hand and, working diligently, progress toward the next rung.

Discomfort. Now we're starting to feel tension. As we discussed in the Pillar Principle of Courage, the Call of the Comfortable often tempts us to quit. At the Discomfort level, we experience pain. We expend finite energy. We're being stretched beyond our comfort zone. But we persevere and keep progressing upward on the ladder of Learning, often because the coaches in our lives believe in us and encourage us to commit to Excellence.

Skill. Now we're able to apply our newly gained knowledge. We've moved from knowing what to do to doing what we know, and we're improving. We're having more fun as we keep striving to perfect our skills. We are performing well, but it is still at a conscious level, having to think about what we're doing and how to do it. We are seeing results from our efforts. But the next rung, the highest level of performance, is the goal.

Reflex action. This is the peak of learning, and it's the result of what is called "patterning," doing something over and over again. Olympic gold medalists understand this concept well.

Like the gymnasts on the balance beam we mentioned before, we learn from our mistakes as we continue up the Ladder of Learning. Though we may fall off, a coach helps pull us up to this top level by encouraging us to get back on … and on … and on again.

A common, yet perhaps dangerous, example of reflex action is what happens to all of us in driving our vehicles. The day I took my road test in 1974, the examiner tersely instructed me to "pull away from the curb and take it straight down the street." So I pulled away from the curb and took my car straight into the passenger side of an elderly woman's slow-moving 1964 push-button Plymouth Valiant. It was the shortest driver's test in New York state history.

Now, after driving a car for 25 years, I can balance my coffee cup on one knee, change the radio station and talk on the cell phone—all while denying my 16-year-old daughter's request for her own set of wheels.

I'm not saying this is a good thing. I'm just saying that through repetition, the motor of learning, we are able to perform instinctively and naturally, without thinking about the steps involved.

It's clear: A good coach helps us climb the Ladder of Learning and reach the apex—reflex action.

3. Coaches see what we cannot see.

Peter Senge, in *The Fifth Discipline*, tells us, "The eye cannot see itself," and it's absolutely true. We simply cannot know how others perceive our performance. I can't tell you how many times I've tried something new in a talk or made a point in a particular way, with the clear intention of communicating one thing, only to have someone point out that I was, in fact, sending a completely different message.

This is not a reflection on my lack of intelligence—or yours, when the same thing happens to you. It just means, "The eye cannot see itself." We experience life from our own perspectives; we see things through our own filters.

A good coach will give me honest, direct input about how I come across to him and to others. While this feedback may not be easy to receive, once processed and applied, it can contribute immeasurably to my personal and professional growth. I just have to make sure I never "execute" the messenger, the coach.

Where to Find a Coach

Where do we find coaches? All around us. Notice I did not say anything about looking under "C" in the Yellow Pages and paying big consulting fees. Coaching can come from friends, co-workers, our children—almost anyone. The key to getting good coaching is to ask. But you'll probably have to ask twice because most people are reluctant to say anything "negative"—especially to your face.

> "What did you think?"
> "It was great!"
> "What did you *really* think?"
> "Well, ..."
> "All right, I'll call you later and we'll talk."

This does not apply only to speaking, of course. The whole field of executive coaching is booming, and for good reason. People are coming to realize what a difference it makes to have a coach who helps them keep things in perspective and stay on track. On the other hand, sometimes we fail to see the need due to the Exception Excuse, complacency and our inability to see ourselves. When we don't ask how we come across, usually no one tells us.

Just before I began speaking to a group of 100 people in Boston, the corporate training manager conducted some quick research by asking for feedback on a recent training class back at headquarters. A man in his mid-40s named Terry quickly and eagerly raised his hand, happy to volunteer. His opinion of the class was on the "corrective" side, but his observations were specific—and respectful in every way. He was simply answering the question. The trainer thanked him and solicited more comments.

The next person had glowing reports and the third thought the class was the best she'd ever taken. With that, the trainer, in front of everyone, turned to the man who had volunteered the negative observations and said, "Well, Terry, if this trend continues, I'm sure you're just going to want to slip quietly from the room, aren't you?" It got a big laugh from the audience.

I watched Terry. He turned red. He physically closed down. He weakly offered some mumbled remarks in his defense. He was no longer part of the group, and it was sad to watch.

What's sadder yet is that the trainer did not realize his own mistake—and may not to this day. He is a man I know and respect, who cares deeply about the people and the organization. But in one moment he made a bad choice—something we all have done and will do again.

Unless the trainer realized his mistake by reflecting back on the situation, the only way he would understand the impact of his comment would be if someone told him. And chances are, no one would have unless he asked—twice. In this situation, he may have needed to ask more than twice, since 100 people had just observed how he handled honest feedback!

While feedback would have been helpful to the training manager, we need to be aware that feedback is not synonymous with coaching. Most of what we get by asking those around us is *feedback,* quick sound bytes of input, which can be helpful. But it's one thing to have information, and another thing entirely to know what to do with it. That's why all seven skills of coaching are so critical. They help us help others *apply* their new knowledge and use it to bring about lasting change in their lives.

I get a lot of helpful feedback from Karen and friends, associates and customers, but few of them have the specific skills David has. (If you'd like to get in touch with David, give me a call.) It's good, if possible, to find someone—whether a paid professional or a friend, colleague or family member—who has some expertise in the area for which you are seeking advice.

If you're a manager, executive or professional of any kind, consider paying a professional coach. Every dollar you spend is a worthwhile investment in your own Excellence, and therefore in your own future. If you are in a position to help others achieve Excellence, consider making yourself available to help others by developing the skills of effective coaching presented in this chapter. You'll find the benefits of *being* a coach are as great as the benefits of *having* one.

Making Excellence Personal

Some questions to help us embrace the Pillar of Excellence:

1. In what way do I manifest the "Who said I need to improve?" posture?

2. How can I eliminate defensive thinking?

3. Which of the seven criteria for an effective coach do I need to develop first?

4. How good am I at helping others celebrate their achievements?

5. In which areas of my life do I want to attain Excellence?

6. Who are some possible coaches I can enlist for my own journey in Excellence?

Pillar Principle Five: Ownership

I was speaking to a group of managers from Medtronic, the medical device manufacturer. After the talk, a man introduced himself to me as John Bowenkamp. John and I got to talking about the many changes in the health-care industry. As the conversation went on, I came to see that John was a truly unique individual.

"Last year I went out to study our angioplasty business in California and I saw the changes that were already happening out there," he said. "I was convinced they would come our way. And I knew we had to do something to prepare for those changes." What he was really saying was that he had some vision and the Courage to act on that vision.

"Our clients are going to do their best to turn our products into commodities," he went on, "and that's what all customers everywhere want to do. Then it's just a price game. The buyers, of course, think that's better for them, but it certainly is bad for us."

I asked him to continue. By now, I was taking notes.

"If the market can define you as merely a vendor rather than a partner, they'll fix a price tag on you based on where they can get your product or service for less. I can't afford to let my clients do that to me. Now, I know my business is still about relationships. I just need a whole lot more of them—inside my hospitals, inside my buying groups and inside my customer organizations. And it's my job to build them!"

That was some pretty astute and accountable thinking. John went on to tell me that because of the changes occurring in his world, he also felt a strong personal need to keep learning, changing and growing himself for the better. What a great illustration of the Pillar of Learning. I was really starting to like this guy.

Right then, his manager, a regional vice president with the company, approached, and proceeded to tell me all about John and his accomplishments. At that, John looked embarrassed, which only reinforced my sense that he wasn't one to suffer from the, "I have arrived!" syndrome. With all of his drive, talent and success, he was still a genuinely humble person.

I finally asked him what might have seemed an off-the-wall question, "John, why do you do all this—taking risks, building relationships with all types of new customers, learning and growing personally— why do you do it?" I'll never forget his answer:

"Because I *own* this company!"

Medtronic is a multi-billion dollar, public corporation and John doesn't own it. But he thinks and acts as if he does, and that's what makes him such a unique individual. I couldn't help but think what a tremendous asset he is to the organization.

Our fifth Pillar Principle, Ownership, is not about being a literal owner, it's about thinking and acting the way an owner thinks and acts. Owners know they have to make things happen. Owners look at those around them and think, Your problem is my problem, too. They ask, "What can I do to make a difference?" People who think like owners make a powerful difference.

Moving Mountains

I was speaking in Bismarck, North Dakota, and on the van ride from the hotel back to the airport, one of the hotel's owners was driving. I asked him, "How many owners are there?"

"Two," he said.

"And how many people work for the organization in total?"

"Fifty-three," he said, which for some reason reminded me of an old joke:

Q: "How many people work with you?"

A: "About half!"

I asked him, "What would it be like if there were 53 people who thought like the two owners?"

His eyes glazed over as he pondered the implications of my question. The owner is the one who comes in early, works hard, finishes the job, takes out the trash and deposits the money. After a few moments of imagining 53 such partners, he said in an awed half-whisper, "Wow! We could move mountains!"

The Pillar—Not the Pride—of Ownership

For many people, the word Ownership speaks of possessing something—the pride of Ownership. Take my first car, for example. It was a 1962 Rambler. I bought it myself for $200 in 1974. It had five speeds on the column and six-inch holes in the seat cushions. I was 16. Do you think I saw perfection? You bet!

I also saw a car I would have great fun driving and working on, constantly. I remember recruiting my mom, who had achieved Excellence at sewing, to attach some old, gold-colored hand towels to the gray seat cushions so I wouldn't fall through the seats and into the more dangerous holes in the floor. Looking back, I'm not sure why I didn't just put my feet through those holes and drive like the Flintstones drive, to save on precious gas money. I loved that car. It wasn't pretty, but I could say with confidence, "It's mine!"

The pride of Ownership is a wonderful feeling. But the Pillar of Ownership does not concern the material things we own as much as it concerns problems, situations and results. It also speaks to opportunities for improvement. Like a good baseball player coming in under a fly ball, owners see a problem and say, "It's mine! I've got it!" Or, in QBQ form, "What can I do to solve the problem? How can I improve this situation?"

If you want to make a difference, look at the problems, issues and challenges around you, think as an owner would and say, "It's mine! I've got it."

Ownership and Service

Ownership is really the ultimate expression of Personal Accountability, so it's no surprise that we would see it reflected in the other Pillars, as we saw other Pillars connected to the Pillar of Courage. When I think of Ownership, the other Pillar I associate with it most strongly is Service. People who take Ownership of the problems and opportunities around them become truly effective servant-leaders. And of course, the opposite also is true. People who don't take Ownership don't serve people well at all.

I was in Birmingham, Alabama, one morning, standing in the lobby of my hotel talking to two hotel staff people. "Ah, excuse me. I need to get to State Farm's building across the street, but since it's raining cats and dogs and I'm carrying about 200 handouts for a speaking engagement, I was wondering if one of you might have two minutes to drive me across the road, please?"

To my utter surprise, they both looked at me and said, in unison, "No. We can't leave the desk," and the look they gave me said, "Who do you think you are? That's not in my job description. How dare you!"

So there I was, feeling underserved, when, fortunately, another customer overheard the exchange and said, "I have a rental car. Let *me* take you."

Now, I'm not necessarily saying the staff should have abandoned their post, but they didn't seem interested even in *trying* to help. "That's not my job. You're on your own!" was the message.

How hard would it have been to at least think, What can I do? Maybe someone there had a car, or some other solution could have been discovered. Maybe they wouldn't have come up with anything, but if they had thought like owners and at least showed me they cared, I'm sure I would have felt more positive about the situation. Like you, as a customer all I'm looking for is a little Ownership.

I checked into a Scottsdale, Arizona, conference resort around ten o'clock one night, for an engagement at eight o'clock the next morning in front of 300 sales professionals. After scoping out the ballroom, I realized I'd be speaking from a fairly high platform. Knowing the audience would probably all be wearing brightly shined penny loafers themselves, I approached the person behind the counter and asked, "Any chance I can get my shoes polished here tonight?"

"Well, Mr. Miller, unless you need your shoes while you sleep, here's what I can do. I'll run down to the drugstore and buy some polish because I don't believe we have any here. Or, a bell person could take them over to a resort across the highway where they have a shoeshine stand that's open until midnight. Or, I could take them home with me, polish them at my house and bring them back around seven a.m. when I start my next shift. Would any of these options be satisfactory for you, Mr. Miller?"

Can you imagine? How would you have responded? "Fantastic! Thanks!"

If she had suggested those options to you, how would you feel about her and her resort? Would you remember her name? Would you be out telling all your friends about her and her establishment? Yes, I'm sure you would.

Well, I'm sorry to let you down, but it never happened—at least not that way. Take a wild guess what I was told when I asked, "Any chance I can get my shoes polished here tonight?"

"Nope. We don't shine shoes."

Once again: no Ownership, no Service. Whatever your position or situation, don't let this happen to any of your "customers," whoever they may be. Think as an owner thinks. Ask yourself QBQs such as, "What can I do to solve the problem?" and "How can I contribute right now?" When you ask these questions, you'll feel the difference Ownership makes.

A Poor Sailor Blames the Wind

Have you heard the saying, "A poor sailor blames the wind?" I've always liked it because the image of someone sitting in a sailboat, stalled out in the middle of a lake, cursing the wind (or lack of it in this case), paints a clear picture of the futility of Blame. I've heard other variations I like too: "A poor worker blames the tools." And thinking back to the Excellence chapter and the story about Bobby, we see clearly, "A poor coach blames the players." Let's have some fun and extend this idea further.

A poor teacher blames the _____.

A poor salesperson blames the _____.

A poor parent blames the _____.

A poor manager blames the _____.

A poor employee blames the _____.

It's pretty easy to fill in those blanks, isn't it? I'm sure this is in part because we recognize the pairings but also because we see it every day. We discussed Blame and finger-pointing in Part 1, but we can see it everywhere we turn, and Blame is the opposite of Ownership. Said differently, Ownership is the antidote to Blame. Owners don't play the Blame Game. They seek solutions instead. They have the "Can do!" and "Will do!" mindset that every organization requires.

Bea Graczyk is vice president of operations at Hutchinson Technology. I once asked her this question: "Bea, over 25 years you've seen a lot of people come and go. Tell me, what is the difference between those who achieve and those who struggle?" I loved her answer.

"Achievers focus on fixing problems; those who struggle spend their time affixing Blame!"

Owners simply tackle an issue, face a challenge or confront a problem rather than asking "Whodunit?" questions and blaming others. So with a tip of the hat to Bea, here's my definition of Ownership:

A decision of the head, heart and hands to fix *the problem and never again* affix *the blame*

By "head, heart and hands," I mean not only do I think about this decision (head), but I feel it (heart) and, most importantly, I do it (hands). I make a personal, gut-level commitment to make a difference and not seek a scapegoat. "Fix the problem and never again affix the Blame." That's Ownership. Blame should never be the objective. Instead we should make the decision, resolve the issue and move the organization, our team and ourselves forward.

Good sailors know the lack of a strong wind is not the problem. And Blame gets them nowhere. If they take it upon themselves to do the work and trim the sails properly, they'll generate forward motion and experience the joy that comes from sailing the open waters. Be a good sailor. Think like an owner.

An Ownership Test

I was scheduled to meet a client for lunch in the upscale restaurant of a fine hotel. What a beautiful place! It had a huge, grand lobby with towering trees, majestic statues and sparkling fountains. I was ten minutes early, so I posted myself in a strategic position on an elegant, very comfortable couch, where I could see both the restaurant and the hotel entrance.

As I waited, I noticed a young housekeeping staff person polishing the brass handrails on the short steps leading into the restaurant. There were three railings and she was working on the far left one, while a line of customers lined up along the freshly polished right-hand railing.

Now, before I continue, let me ask you this: What's a handrail for? It's to hold on to, right? Well, that's exactly what the three men in line at the time were doing as they waited for their table: chatting, laughing and dragging their hands across the freshly polished railing.

Have you ever had one of those moments in which you see something coming and you're thinking, No, this is not going to happen! Well, it did. I can still see the picture in my mind of this young housekeeper down on her knees with her hair tied up in a bun and a glint of perspiration shining on her forehead, looking up at those three men, her three customers, and saying, "Excuse me. Would you please take your hands off those railings. I just polished them!"

To my utter surprise, these three fairly large, power-suited guys quickly let go of the railing and jumped back in total shock! But then in a sharp tone, one of them asked her the same question I asked you: "Well, what's a railing for?"

Now, here's the test: You're her manager and you happened to be sitting next to me on the couch and saw the whole thing. What will you do? Will you ask the wrong questions such as, "When will she get it?" "Why doesn't she care?" "When will she serve the customers better?" and "Why isn't she motivated?"

Or will you take Ownership of the situation and ask yourself questions such as, "What can I do to be a better coach for her?" and "How can I help her understand her customers better?" If it's the latter, you pass the test. Taking Ownership is the better way to manage and live, no matter what your position.

The Power of Small Acts

Like a lot of people, I enjoy a good bagel in the morning. I entered a well-known bagel shop one morning and ordered a salt bagel with cream cheese, and as an afterthought added, "Oh, may I have my bagel toasted, please?"

Without looking up, the person helping me said, "We don't toast bagels."

More out of curiosity than anything else, I said, "I'd think a lot of people would like their bagels toasted in the morning."

At that he stopped his work mid-slice and said sternly, "Sir, if I toasted your bagel, I'd have *everybody* in here wanting toasted bagels!"

Would that be so bad, a place full of people? Might even make for a good marketing campaign: "We toast your bagels when nobody else will!"

The funny thing about this to me is that I know there's more to the story. I know the problem is not just this one guy in this particular store. Somewhere off in the mountains, I can just picture the executives of this company out on a retreat with their high-priced marketing guru and their flip charts, pondering the question, "How do we get more customers into our stores?" That may sound cynical, but I've facilitated too many executive workshops to be told any different. This kind of thing happens all the time. Corporate is saying one thing while the field is doing something quite different.

How does this tie into Ownership? Sometime during the executive retreat, as they commune and commiserate, someone invariably will say, "When will *the people* catch the vision?"

Meanwhile, in the field, the non-bagel-toasting employee who is essentially telling customers with special requests to go away, is also inquiring, "When will *they* share the vision?" Both groups are contributing to the same problem while blaming each other for the breakdown. It's a sad situation that could be turned around in a heartbeat with the Pillar of Ownership. If everybody involved simply embraced this idea, how much better would things be, everywhere?

This idea of taking Ownership doesn't only apply to one group or another. It's for me and you and everyone else—top to bottom, front line to head office.

Most of the examples of a lack of Ownership we've discussed have been little things. In and of themselves, they're not earth-shattering events. One customer here, two or three there. But think for a moment what the larger implications might be for you and your organization. In how many little ways are customers being disappointed every day? How many disappointments will it take before they go somewhere else for good? What are they telling their friends about us? What is it costing us all in productivity, competitive edge, morale and employee turnover?

Taken individually, these failings may be small things, but taken together, the impact is tremendous. We all need to start taking Ownership and we need to do it now.

QBQ Ownership

The Pillar of Ownership, like so much of what we've talked about, comes down to the choices we make in the moment. At the point of frustration, we may be tempted to ask the IQ, "When will my people live the vision?" It's far more productive, however, if instead we stop ourselves and ask the QBQ, "What can I do to more effectively communicate the vision to our people?" or "How can I elicit their involvement in creating a shared vision?"

By asking QBQs, we transfer our energy from Procrastination, Blame and Victim Thinking into action and Personal Accountability. Imagine what we could accomplish in our organizations and our lives if we all came to work every day and demonstrated Ownership by asking the QBQ, "What can I do?" Not long ago, I found out what just one person could accomplish.

I was speaking on the QBQ in a three-hour interactive session. We had roughly 60 people in the company cafeteria, seated at round tables, about six to a table. The discussion groups were made up of actual working teams from the unionized shop floor. We had lots of conversation that day on how and why to apply the QBQ within the organization for a positive impact on their culture.

When the session was over, the director of manufacturing was in front thanking everyone for attending. Suddenly, out of the blue, a woman named Sally stood up, interrupted her supervisor and said in a strong, sure voice, "I want Teams 1, 3 and 7 to stay behind for a while. We need to stop the blaming that's happening around the new project, OK?"

Fifty-nine people stared in total silence. They were as impressed as I was, and hope you are, by her courageous act of Ownership. I looked at Tables 1, 3 and 7, and their heads were nodding in agreement. They stayed behind and I did, too. For another half-hour, they talked about taking Ownership and eliminating Blame. Good for them and good for Sally. She decided to take Ownership by becoming a Blame Buster. What a difference!

With just one act of Ownership, Carl Esterhay, the Millers' financial adviser at Norwest, made a lasting difference. A few years ago, a major corporate client was coming to see Carl for a meeting. When the client arrived, he happened to mention to Carl that he hadn't parked in the Norwest lot, but on the street at a two-hour meter.

Later, the meeting was running long and Carl, thinking about the client's meter, excused himself and slipped away. As Carl put it, this man may have been worth millions, but no one wants a parking ticket, no matter what his income.

Not knowing what kind of car the man drove, or exactly where he'd parked, Carl had a problem. Oh well, what the heck, you only live once, he thought. He stopped at the bank on the main floor, got enough quarters to break an elephant's back, and hit the street on a cold, windy winter day. He plugged the meters of every car in the area, staying just one step ahead of the "meter monsters."

It was a bold thing to do, but he got the job done and no one got a ticket, including, as he later discovered, the important client. And it seems the client found out about Carl's actions as well.

"How much did that cost you?" I asked him.

"Just over $90," he said, with a hint of "ask me more" in his voice.

I continued, "Do you feel it was worth it?"

Carl smiled and said playfully, "Go ahead, ask me if that man *was* my customer!"

I played along, "OK, *was* that multi-millionaire with tons of money to invest, your customer?"

He smiled, winked and said, "No, but he is now!"

And I'd bet all of Carl's quarters, and then some, he will be for life. Why? Carl made his customer's problem *his* problem. He took Ownership. If someone had taken care of you that way, wouldn't you seriously consider becoming his customer too? I know I would. Ownership makes the difference.

I have a friend named Tana who also illustrates the personal benefits of taking Ownership. Tana used to sell home building products to contractors. She was so excited when she first started, fresh out of college, ready to begin her new sales career. On her first day, though, she was assigned the territory no one else wanted. On her second day, she was handed a list of 20 names and numbers to contact, and the list was titled, "Dead Accounts"!

Dead accounts, of course, are those potential customers someone else has decided will never buy. No one had been able to sell them anything, so they gave them to Tana.

She went to her new colleagues, hoping for some ideas and support, but quickly found out they didn't have any time for her. They were too busy complaining about their own situations.

She went to her manager for some coaching, and he happily took her through the entire training program, which, it turned out, consisted of two sentences: "You can do it! Go out there and get 'em!" Have you ever received—or delivered—that coaching program?

There she was, with dead accounts and no help from her peers or her manager. What's a person to do? I guess we all know the behaviors she *could* have chosen: Blame, Procrastination, Victim Thinking. "Who's going to help me out?" (Blame) "When is someone going to train me?" (Procrastination) "Why did they give me the crummy territory?" (Victim Thinking)

In Tana's situation, with all she had going against her, it would have been easy to think and feel that way, and I don't think anyone would have thought poorly of her for it, either. She was in a tough spot.

But she didn't choose any of those paths. She chose instead to think and act like an owner and make a difference. "How can I contribute value to my customers today" and "What actions can I take to make a difference?" She didn't sit around feeling sorry for herself, pointing fingers or waiting for her customers to come to her. She simply picked up the phone and made the calls. One year later, Tana had more than nine-hundred thousand dollars in revenue from the original list of 20 dead accounts!

That's quite an accomplishment. And I know she felt great about it. But beyond that, how do you think she felt about herself? Embracing the Pillar of Ownership helps us make a real difference in our organizations and our lives. That holds true regardless of who we are or what our position may be.

A Little Piece of Heaven

Minnesota, which is not known for its balmy winters in the first place, had a stretch of particularly discouraging weather in January 1992. For 17 straight days there was no sunshine at all, nothing but thick, gloomy clouds.

In the midst of all that, Ted Deikel, chairman and CEO of Fingerhut Companies, Inc., demonstrated a masterful bit of Ownership thinking. He saw the effect the weather was having on his people and instead of focusing on something he clearly couldn't control, he thought, Well, what can I do?

Ted asked his executive team to select about one-hundred people and tell them to be at the Minneapolis/St Paul International Airport early the next morning. When they arrived, Ted loaded them all onto a chartered plane and flew everyone up above the clouds for a morning of spirit-lifting sunshine!

Isn't that amazing? Instead of saying something such as, "Come on! What's wrong with you folks? You can't let the weather get you down. We've got work to do!" he sent the message, "I care about you. Let's go for a ride!" and his people heard it loud and clear.

If you worked for Fingerhut, how would Ted's action help you feel about the company? And what's that worth to someone in Ted's position? You can't put a price on it. Also, though his original thinking was, What can I do, right here, right now to help out?, the goodwill from that gesture spread far beyond. For years after, people would say to a Fingerhut employee at a party or picnic, "Wow, you work for Fingerhut? Isn't that the company that took a group up in a plane to enjoy the sunshine? Must be a terrific organization to work for!" The goodwill was priceless. Combining Ownership thinking with decisive action is a powerful thing indeed.

Was it a risk? Sure. And chartering a plane for that many people is not cheap, either. But when you think of all the impact that one act had on the business, I'll bet it was some of the best money Ted ever invested!

Making Ownership Personal

We started our discussion on the Pillar of Ownership talking about John Bowenkamp, who said, "I own this company!" We can say it another way: "How can I contribute toward solving the problem?"

I leave us all with this challenge: Let's identify an issue, problem or dilemma that we've ignored, waited for someone else to handle or felt sorry for ourselves over, and go forth today to make a positive difference. With Ted, Tana, Carl, Sally and John as our models, let's do it now and reap the rewards a life of Ownership can bring.

As you consider these real-life examples, ask:

1. What can I do today to move my organization forward?

2. How can I not only raise an issue, but solve the problem?

3. What situation have I avoided, in which my energy and talent could make a positive difference right now?

4. What action will I take today to demonstrate Ownership?

Pillar Principle Six: Creativity

About ten years ago, when I was with The Fortune Group selling training to corporations, Bob Bonkiewicz joined our sales team. Bob is a great guy and he has a unique selling style. He would go on sales calls carrying two items: a Crayola marking pen (not a crayon, but close) and a legal tablet. His total investment: two bucks, max.

Once comfortable in the office of a vice president or the CEO, Bob would take his fancy tools out of his well-worn briefcase and go to work. He would draw a circle in the upper left corner of his yellow pad, write the word "Leadership" in it and say, "We work in the area of leadership development." Then he'd draw another circle, write "Selling Skills" in it and say, "We work in the area of Sales Training." He would do the same with "Team Building" and so on.

After drawing five or six circles, Bob would slide the legal tablet across the desk and engage in the secret of selling. How did he do that? He would look at the customer with great sincerity and ask a QBQ, "How can I help you the most?"

Using this simple approach, not only did Bob win "Rookie of the Year," he also sold more training in his first year than any one else ever had! That's great selling, and I think Bob, with his Crayola marker and legal tablet, demonstrates how we've over-complicated the whole business of selling and communicating by adding endless techniques, strategies and tactics.

Bob is also an excellent example of our sixth Pillar Principle, Creativity. Normally when we think of Creativity, we think of artistic skills such as writing, drawing or painting. In the business world, we hear a lot about "thinking outside the box," which expresses the idea that breaking old paradigms and changing our perspectives on things can help us find new and creative ways of doing things. But clients have told me the problem with thinking outside the box is that too often it gets translated into, "We have to have some new stuff." In other words, "We can't do our jobs without the latest tools and technologies."

Breaking old paradigms can help us discover new realities, but many solutions do not require that we go outside the box. More money, newer equipment, fresh products and better supplies do not automatically solve problems. Sometimes, like Bob, we just need to take a fresh look at the tools we already have. While thinking outside the box may help us generate some new ideas, my favorite definition of Creativity is this:

Succeeding within *the box*

Bob didn't ask these IQs: "When are we going to get a four-color brochure like the one Wilson Learning has?" or "Why don't we have the beautiful marketing materials of a Dale Carnegie training company?"

Instead, he asked the QBQ of Creativity: "What can I do to succeed with the tools and resources I already have?" That's a powerful question and that's why he was so successful.

More Stuff, Better Stuff, New Stuff!

When we ask for more stuff, we sound like our children, don't we? If they're like a lot of children, they're constantly asking for "stuff." Sometimes—perhaps often—we give in and get them more stuff. Then what do they want? More stuff!

I know I've fallen into the trap of thinking, "I can't do my job without more stuff!" More budget dollars, a cell phone, sample products for the trunk of my car, lower pricing, advertising, leads, training, all kinds of computer stuff. The list goes on and on. "I have to have more stuff!" And I'm not the only one.

The vice president of marketing for a large manufacturing organization once said to me, "It's funny, John. Whenever people in our sales force make a big sale, it's always due to terrific tactics and smooth selling. But when they miss a sale, it's because of the lack of support and materials from the marketing department!" More stuff! Better stuff!

And any sales manager worth her salt knows that the salespeople who struggle are the ones seeking to sell the next product—the one not yet produced—because the ones they have in their bag aren't competitive any more. They're just not good enough, at least not in their minds. Better stuff! New stuff!

Remember Stephanie, the receptionist from the chapter on Service who said, "I'm so thankful you held for me," and then told me she'd been hired away by another firm? Well, when I met with the president of her organization that day, he asked this IQ, "Why can't we get good people?" He thought he needed new stuff too—new people. But that wasn't his problem. His QBQ could have been, "How can I develop and appreciate the people we have?"

Success is not the product of more stuff, better stuff or new stuff. It's the product of Creativity!

Tools and Territories

I'll never forget the time I shared the story about Bob Bonkiewicz at a session for AmerUs Life Insurance in Des Moines, Iowa. A young agent ran up to me afterward and said something I hadn't heard before, "Well, John, you got me. You got me good!"

"I got you? What do you mean by that?" I asked him.

"For the last six months, I've been bugging my boss for a bigger, faster, stronger laptop computer." Then he proudly held up a legal tablet and said, "But today I learned I can succeed with this!"

That man had learned because he had changed. Changed what? His thinking and the way he views himself. Before the conference he had been saying, "I can't sell without new tools," and after the conference he was saying, "Well, it might be a bit tougher, but I believe I *can* do the job without the laptop. How can I achieve with what I have?" What a shift in thinking!

In some jobs, territories are more important than tools, which brings us to another excuse that kills our Creativity, one you'll never hear from the lips of a practitioner of this Pillar Principle. I call them the Ten Terrible Words: "... but Boss, my territory is *different* from all the others!"

Tom Sween told me about a customer service representative who delivered food items to small retailers and convenience stores. He wanted his old route back. Tom is the CEO and owner of E.A. Sween Company, an extremely well managed and successful food distribution firm. The rep's route was a specific geographic area he had actually asked to leave. He now was asking for it to be returned to him, the rightful owner, because, in his words, "It's obviously bigger now!"

In reality, it was just producing more revenue—in fact, according to Tom, much more revenue. Why? Because the new person working the territory, instead of complaining, "... but Boss, my territory is *different* from all the others!" was practicing the Pillar of Creativity by asking a QBQ or two. In other words, he was asking questions that begin with "What" or "How," contain an "I" and focus on action.

What's happening in your territory and mine? We don't need to be in sales to have a "territory," you know. Is our effectiveness—the impact we're having on our territories and our world—growing?

I hope so and I know it can, but only when we engage in Creativity. Take another look at the tools and resources already available to you. I'll bet if you apply a little Creativity, you'll find new ways to succeed within the box.

Succeed to Get What You Need

I was conducting a session on Creativity and the QBQ, and my friend Michael DeVito was there. At one point, Michael was saying that he agreed with the thoughts on Creativity presented and that he had learned from his own experience that he needed to do the job with the tools available. Someone at his discussion table said they admired him for his conviction. Michael stopped them and said, "Don't give me any credit, please. It's not as if I'm Mr. Enlightened. I just realized I was burning myself out asking for things I would never get!"

I know another group who would agree with that. Right before I spoke to the Philadelphia subsidiary of an Indianapolis-based financial organization, the president of the company got up to report on his recent meeting with the company's owners. He told the group that he had presented a number of issues to the executives, including his request to triple the advertising budget.

After he concluded his remarks and sat down, one of the salespeople raised her hand and said, "Bruce, you never told us—did we get the additional advertising funds?" He walked back up to the lectern, paused, looked out over the group, and with his characteristic dry sense of humor, said, "No, but I brought back a whole bunch more corporate sympathy!" The crowd roared. They got the message: Succeed with what you have.

Am I saying we should never ask for new tools and materials? Not at all. It's very healthy and productive to talk about and explore any resources we could use to make a difference. We can still recommend, request and lobby for whatever we feel we need to do our jobs: laptops, budget dollars, cell phones, four-color brochures, people or new technology.

But I want to make this crystal clear: What truly fuels Creativity is asking the QBQ, "How can I accomplish the goal with what I have?" Successful people manage to get the job done with what's before them. The creative person says, "I can achieve my goals with the stuff I have now!"

Wishing and waiting for magic solutions are common ways to avoid practicing Personal Accountability. Blaming the territory, the competition or other entities beyond our control—departments, distributors, suppliers or individuals—never resolves problems or overcomes obstacles. All that happens, as Michael expressed so well, is that we get burned out from continually asking for what we don't have. We waste precious time and energy.

When we change our thinking and start looking for creative ways to succeed within the box, not only do we become more productive, life becomes more fun!

The reality is that we could probably use more tools and there might never be enough. Let's save ourselves the frustration of asking all the time and focus on what we can do with what we have.

And the beauty of it is—well, I'll let Deb tell you. Deb Weber is a client of mine and a middle manager at State Farm Insurance. We were talking about the topic of Creativity one day and she said, "What I've learned is that every time I do my job well and reach the objective with the tools I already have, *I end up getting more tools.*" So if we get our focus off the tools we want and practice succeeding with the tools we have, we may just get the tools we wanted in the first place!

Creativity and the QBQ

Earlier, I mentioned my client, St. Jude Medical. St. Jude is a cash-rich organization, and I'd be a lot richer too, had I bought their stock when I first started calling on them in 1986. Even though they're a wealthy company, I can still tell you there are definite spending limits at St. Jude Medical, as there should be. There's no Carte Blanche at St. Jude.

I made a comment to that effect during a session at Land O'Lakes, an agriculture-based cooperative and one of their people said, "You know, John, if St. Jude Medical has $10 in the budget, we probably have a dollar!" I imagine that's true. In facilitating a QBQ program for the non-profit Campfire Boys and Girls I was told that if St. Jude has $10 and Land O'Lakes has $1, the Campfire Boys and Girls might have 10 cents. One thin dime.

Resources can be tight anywhere. At the same time, every one of those groups is succeeding and doing great things. And they're doing them with the resources they have by asking QBQs such as, "How can I achieve my goals with what I have before me?"

In reality, when we say, "Why don't I get more tools to do my job?" what we're really saying is, "Someone outside of me owns my achievement!" In the chapter on Ownership, we discussed how we need to take Ownership for problems and opportunities to achieve and succeed. But when we say, "When am I going to get more tools?" we're not taking Ownership of our situation. Essentially we're saying, "If I don't meet the objective, finish the project on time or sell my quota, it's *your* fault because you wouldn't give me more tools." That's the complete opposite of Personal Accountability, and it's a dead-end road. Thinking differently, asking QBQs and embracing the Pillar of Creativity can be our edge.

Personal Accountability and Creativity

Karen and I have a tool we use to help teach our kids about Creativity and the tough choices often required to practice Personal Accountability. It's a cash budget system. I'll get to the Creativity part in a moment, but first I thought you might enjoy hearing a little about the system.

Each month, our kids get a specified amount of money not connected with chores. (Household jobs are done by each "team member" because this family is a team, and all must contribute.) When they receive their money, it's divided into five categories using "cash envelopes." Kristin started on the plan at nine, Tara, seven, and Mike and Molly, age six. The categories are savings, charitable giving, gifts (for birthdays and holidays), miscellaneous and clothing. Yes, clothing. Kristin and Tara—not Mom and Dad—for many years now have bought their own jeans, shirts, dress clothes, winter coats, shoes and gymnastics outfits.

There are a couple of keys to making the system work. First, when the dollars transfer from our hands to our children's, the money belongs to them. We can coach a bit as they learn and grow, but if they want to buy "junk" that we know in three days will be lost under the couch with the dust bunnies, they can buy it. It's their money. The hardest lesson for us all-knowing, omnipotent parents to learn is that it's *their* money.

Secondly, as our kids will tell you, "When it's gone, it's *gone!*" It doesn't matter if there's "too much month at the end of the money." When Molly first started getting her wad, she'd blow it fast. After a few months, since she couldn't really comprehend the value of a dollar, when she was considering a purchase in the store, she'd turn and ask,

"Dad, what day of the month is it?" because she knew: When it's gone, it's gone.

And finally, parents must understand the purpose of the budget system. The purpose is not for the children to learn to handle money. That's an important benefit, of course, but the true purpose of the program is to teach the essential skill of decision making. We want our kids to develop the ability to make a decision and stand by the consequences of that choice. Frankly, I wish I had learned it at a younger age myself.

We know the system works because we watch our teenage girls go to J.C. Penney for clothing instead of to the more upscale stores. On top of that, there's no reaching into Mom's purse for the plastic money and no arguments with Dad over how much money they should receive on a trip to the mall for clothes. They have their own money, there are limits and everyone knows what they are. Now, here's the story that truly demonstrates the impact this system has on Creativity.

The girls, coming back from camp, asked to be driven to the Target store because they'd enjoyed playing a game called Catch Phrase and they thought it would be lots of fun to play it with their family and friends. We went to the store, found the game and studied the price tag. It was the 27th of the month and between the two of them, they were about six dollars short. Not once did they look to me. They knew better. I'm not a cruel person, but for me to step in and lend or give them the money would have destroyed the integrity of the budget system.

So we went home, a bit disappointed. Then Creativity kicked in. I started hearing laughter from the other room. The girls would appear in the kitchen for supplies and quickly disappear again. Whatever they were doing, they were having fun. Any idea what was going on?

From scrap supplies, they created the Miller version of Catch Phrase, and for the next two hours, we sat around the coffee table and enjoyed each other's company as we played the game.

I don't think it ever would have occurred to me to make our own version of that game, but the two girls were undeterred by their lack of resources. They put their heads together, practiced Creativity and came up with a solution.

The Power of One

After a 25-year career in parenting, Judy Wolf decided to pursue a different job. She searched around and found a position as a cashier at the Home Depot.

One morning, when she had been on the job a few weeks, a young man came through her line, obviously in a hurry. He quickly plunked down a few items and a $100 bill, but the total only came to $2.89.

"Do you have anything smaller?" Judy asked him.

"No, I'm sorry, this is all I have," he said. At that moment, Judy had a choice to make.

Since she had just opened up for the day, she only had forty dollars in the drawer. That meant she would have to send his $100 bill up through a pneumatic tube to the front office with a note requesting they break it down for her. But that would take time, of course, which her customer didn't seem to have. Still, what else could she do?

Creativity to the rescue! She handed the young man back his bill, reached down for her purse, took out $2.89, put it in the register, processed the transaction and tore off the receipt. Then she turned to her customer with a smile and said, "Thanks for shopping at the Home Depot!"

"What?" he said, stunned, "Are you sure?"

"Yes, go on. Get out of here," she said. "I can see you've got a lot to do."

Thanks!" he said excitedly, and left. And as far as Judy was concerned, that was the end of it.

Two days later, though, her supervisor, looking both confused and a little amused, approached her holding an envelope and said, "Judy, I need to get this straight. Did you actually *buy* the merchandise for one of our customers the other day?"

She had to think. "Yes. I guess I did."

"Well, they've sent you a tip," he said. "And as a Home Depot employee, I'm sure you know you can't accept tips."

"I don't want a tip." she said. But curiosity got the best of her and she asked, "How much?"

"They wrote you a check for $50."

"Wow! How about if I endorse it and put it in the pizza fund so we can all share it?" she asked.

"OK. We can do that." The money went into the pizza fund and no one thought any more of it.

But the next day, the young man showed up in her line again. This time he had someone else with him, his father, Bob Johnson, Sr., owner of Johnson Construction Company. We never know whom we touch, do we?

The elder Mr. Johnson said to Judy, "I want you to know that because of what you did to serve my son the other day, we've decided to switch our primary supplier from another company to the Home Depot for everything we need."

This is a true story about the power of one—and the power of the QBQ, "How can I contribute?" Don't let it ever be said that one person cannot create value and have impact.

Instead of accepting things as they were, Judy focused on her customer and the resources at her disposal, and asked, "What can I do right now?" instead of asking, "When will the organization change?" She came up with a creative solution with impact far beyond her choice in that moment. That's a lot better than asking, "When are they going to improve the processes and systems around here?" "Why doesn't the customer have smaller bills?" or "Who's going to give me more cash in the drawer?" The results demonstrate the power of choices—and the power of the QBQ.

But we're not quite done with Judy's story. Still at the counter, the younger Mr. Johnson leaned toward Judy and said, in a half-whisper, "Judy, I've got to know."

"You've got to know what?" she whispered back.

"The day you bought my merchandise—how *high* would you have gone?"

Laughing, she said, "Twenty bucks, because that's all I carry in my purse."

I shared that story with the owner of another retail business recently and she said, "I want that person working for me!"

Judy would be a welcome team member anywhere because of the way she thinks. For her, paying a customer's bill rather than making him wait while she carried out company policy was simply the right thing to do in that particular situation. It was also a creative solution to a simple problem. Through her Creativity, Judy demonstrated the Power of One.

When Failure is Not an Option

Do you remember the story of Apollo 13? You probably do. It's a powerful story of Courage, commitment and heroism. It's the story of a team coming together to beat unbeatable odds. It's also a great story of Creativity. You may recall, one of the many crises the crew faced was a potentially fatal problem with the oxygen system. The filtration system wasn't designed to handle the loads they were putting on it and the crew was slowly suffocating.

In the movie, there was a great scene where a team of engineers in Houston gathered around a table and dumped out replicas of all the items the astronauts had in the capsule. They had to come up with some way to put these things together to make a workable filter, and they had to do it quickly.

If I were in this situation, my first thoughts probably would be, Why me? Who got us into this mess in the first place? This is impossible! I can also imagine looking at the pile of stuff on the table and thinking, We need more stuff! But the Apollo 13 team did not. In fact, I don't believe I ever saw a headline that read, "NASA Engineers Ask for More Stuff." They just did the job with what they had. They succeeded *within* the box. Somehow, they rose to the challenge and figured out a way to rig those items together to create a solution, saving the men and the mission.

How about you and me? How's our can-do spirit? What tools and resources are we asking for that we possibly could succeed without? Let's take a fresh look at our situation, think like Bob with his marker and legal tablet, Judy with her $20 in cash and the Apollo engineers with their collection of ordinary items for an extraordinary situation. And let us not focus so much on what we lack. Instead, let's concentrate on the great things we can accomplish with what we have. Let's ask the QBQ, "What can I do to succeed with the tools and resources I already possess?"

Making Creativity Personal

A few questions to help us practice this Pillar:

1. What have I been asking for that I could do without if I asked a better question?

2. How can I adapt to the environment around me and use the tools at my disposal?

3. What task have I been considering too big without new stuff, and how will I tackle that problem now?

4. In what area of my world do I need to employ the definition of Creativity—succeeding *within* the box—today?

Pillar Principle Seven: Trust

The Princess Jasmine is in a perilous situation. For the second time in the movie, Aladdin is there, reaching out to her, stretching, straining, desperately trying to rescue her. But she hesitates, frightened.

Then he looks into her eyes and asks, "Do you trust me?"

In a perfect Disney moment, Jasmine knows the answer. Her fear dissolves as she takes Aladdin's hand. She's safe. And we can breathe again.

"Do you trust me?" It's a question that strikes at the heart of all relationships. To the extent our business relationships are based on mutual trust, business is good. Likewise, when we've built trust in our personal relationships, life is good.

How do we improve our relationships? The simple answer is to increase the level of Trust, which is why we are addressing Trust as a

Pillar Principle. And increasing Trust in a relationship, to a large extent, means improving communication.

You may not perceive a problem with Trust in your organization, but I'll bet you see obvious problems with communication. I say that because in all the years I facilitated leadership training with teams, I'd often open with this question: "What are your critical business issues today?"

Eight out of 10 times, the first answer we put on the flip chart was the "C" word. Not competition, not change, but communication. "Yes," they'd all agree, "our biggest problem is communication!" My hunch is that you've had a similar experience.

Interestingly enough, I've also discovered that, 99 percent of the time, organizations frame their communication problems in the context of an IQ: "When will they communicate better?" This question, of course, shows a total lack of Personal Accountability. But it also indicates a lack of understanding of the link between Trust and communication. The QBQ, as simple as it may sound, is this: "How can I better understand you?"

We will communicate openly only in an environment characterized by Trust. That's because open communication involves risk: the risk of making a mistake, the risk of sounding stupid, the risk of being rejected—sometimes the risk of damaging our careers. If someone doesn't trust they'll be safe, they won't communicate freely and completely.

For example, I was facilitating a workshop for senior managers at a 40-million-dollar company, to help them formulate a new mission statement. At one point, the CEO glared at his six department directors and said in a shaming tone, "Why would you *not* know our current mission statement? It's been on the lobby wall for a year now! When are you people going to get it together?"

In his mind his anger was justified, but in terms of communication, he may have set the organization back years. After beating up his directors emotionally, he could hardly expect them to feel comfortable being frank and honest with him. Could you have been frank and honest under those circumstances?

I actually saw the breakdown in Trust with that very group later in the day when two people said things to me on break I knew they'd never say to the CEO. And the saddest part is, as people leave the organization, that CEO very likely will ask the IQ, "Why can't I get any good people?" when, in fact, he already may have very good people who just don't trust him enough to share their ideas openly with him.

Building Trust

If your organization is like most, you probably have some teams that don't function well, some departments and divisions that compete more than they cooperate, and some people who feel more indicted than inspired. You're right if you diagnose these as communication and relationship problems. The purpose of this chapter is to show that we can start resolving many of those problems by building more Trust within our organizations.

How can we build Trust? First we need to have a good understanding of what it is. On an emotional level, we can identify Trust when we experience it, but allow me to share a good example with you, anyway.

Remember the story from the Pillar of Learning about Stacy and her dad in the airplane with the stalled engine? When she told me the story, I asked her, "Weren't you terrified up there?"

"No," she said, "As I look back on it, I wasn't."

I didn't believe her. "Do you really mean that? You weren't scared at all?"

"No, I really wasn't afraid," she insisted. "I just remember it as an interesting experience. The guy flying the plane was my dad! I didn't feel any fear. Not one bit. Why would I? I *trusted* him."

Now that's a picture of Trust! But what is Trust, really? Where does it come from?

Trust is a State of Mind

The word Trust is used in many different ways, but it's essentially a state of mind, a belief. When I say, "I trust you," what I'm really saying is, "I think I know you well enough to predict your behavior, and your behavior has proved trustworthy in the past. Therefore, I believe you'll act in my best interests. I believe you won't hurt me. I believe you'll do your best not to let me down."

Trust is a delicate state—one that's hard to build and easy to shatter. All it takes is one hurt, one disappointment, one act that doesn't fit our predictions, and we tend to pull back. The moment someone gets the feeling, "I don't know you anymore," Trust is gone.

When we say we know someone, what is it that we know? We never really know what someone is thinking or feeling. We have our opinions and theories, but we don't know for sure. The only things we can be certain of are what we see and hear—in other words, the things people say and do. So for the purpose of our discussion, let's define Trust this way:

Building another's confidence in me through what I say and do

This means simply that if we want to build Trust, we need to consider our actions and our words, and be accountable for their impact. It's true, Trust is a by-product, a result, of the things I say and do. When I understand that, I can ask the right questions, practice Personal Accountability and build Trust-filled relationships.

How to Kill Trust

1. Communicate, "I don't know you."

Robin Peterson, executive vice president of Coldwell Banker Burnet, recalls with laughter how back in the 1970s, early in her real estate career, she was showing a home to a couple and said, "You'll certainly want to get rid of the purple wallpaper, paint and carpet. Yuck!"

The couple was quiet but as they left the house they invited Robin to their home across town. "How nice of them!" she thought, and twenty minutes later she entered their well-kept home. It was decorated in twelve shades of lavender.

As Robin turned twelve shades of red, she knew immediately she wasn't going to make this sale! Right or wrong, intentional or not, they heard her words say loud and clear, "You don't know us and you don't understand us," and that was the end of the relationship.

The "I don't know you, you don't know me" message has a great deal to do with the walls we build between people, teams, departments and locations within our organizations, too. Listen for the underlying messages in these IQs:

"Why doesn't marketing spend some time in the field and find out what's actually going on in the real world?"

"When is accounting going to provide me the information I need when I need it?"

"Who in corporate is going to start sharing the vision with the field?"

"When will the salespeople get off the golf course and execute our programs?"

"Why can't manufacturing make the product the customers want and deliver it when they want it?"

Have you ever heard IQs such as those? What are they really saying? It's possible they simply say "You don't know me" and "I don't understand you." I believe these questions indicate a deep lack of Trust.

On the other hand, I've done workshops in which we put people from different departments in the same room and had them ask each other a question that had rarely, if ever, been asked before, "How can I help you do your job better?" And it is always a pleasure to watch the walls come down—all as a result of a simple QBQ.

2. Communicate, "I don't trust you."

Our actions can communicate clearly a message of Trust or the lack of Trust. The message "I don't trust you"—quite obviously—is a real

Trust killer. Top managers of a major financial institution demonstrated how little they understood this principle when they decided to bolt laptop computers permanently to each person's desk! Can you imagine?

My friend Vince is another example. He had been with the same company for some time and was happy and successful enough. For three consecutive years, his sales were in the top 10 percent in a 50-person sales force.

Then things changed. His company was being acquired by another and, of course, he didn't know what to expect since he didn't know the new owners. His manager began acting out of character, and Vince felt he didn't know him anymore, either.

With Trust fading, Vince made a decision. He took a vacation day and flew to the East Coast to interview with another organization in the same industry. He thought nobody at his company knew he had done this.

When he returned the following day, he entered his office to find his manager waiting for him. The manager let Vince have it. Anger flared and the volume escalated. Vince tried to explain why he had made the trip but his manager—whom he thought he knew so well—wasn't interested in Vince's concerns.

"Why would you embarrass us by interviewing with our competitor?" he asked angrily. With that, he drove the last sense of connection and Trust Vince had left, out the window. The manager's actions and words made it inevitable: Within 30 days, Vince was gone.

This didn't have to happen. If his manager, in spite of his anger and hurt and his fear of losing a top sales person, had made a different choice, things might have worked out differently. The action he neglected to take was to use a QBQ and ask, "What can I do to help you reach *your* goals?" Had he done that, Vince very well might have stayed, because that question, that action, would have built his confidence in his manager, increasing mutual Trust.

QBQ Trust

One of my three mentors, Jim Strutton, whom you met in the chapter on Excellence, used to say to me, "John, if the customer does not understand the value of your product, if the customer is not sharing her critical business issues with you, if the customer is not taking the actions he should take, it's not the customer's problem! It's *your* problem. It's your job to build the trusting relationship!"

He was right. Trust is a two-way street, but it starts with me. I was taught that communication never begins with being understood. It always begins with *understanding* the other person. If I want more Trust, I have to start acting and speaking differently. I need to take Personal Accountability for the amount of Trust in the relationship and start sending more messages that say, "I care about you, I want to know more about you." This can be done by asking the QBQ, "How can I better understand you?" When we ask this question, it makes a huge difference.

After speaking in Orlando for the General Motors Service Parts Operations group, a man named Danny came up to me in the back of the ballroom and said, "Wow, the QBQ message sums up the past year for me!" I asked him to explain and he told me he had wanted to leave the organization about a year earlier. He had been asking IQs such as, "Why do they make my job so difficult?" and "When will they change?" Finally, he announced his resignation to his regional manager, Frank.

The short story is that he didn't officially quit. On the day we met, he had been back just four weeks from a one-year leave of absence. He excitedly told me what he'd done during that year: He virtually had completed a masters degree in business, passed the Series 7 exam in case he ever wanted to be a stock broker, and was within four hours of a pilot's license. All in one year! When I expressed my amazement, he gave credit to both Frank and Tom.

"Who's Tom?" I asked. "Oh, he's Frank's boss, the area manager. When Tom learned I was quitting, he recommended to Frank and me that I take the 12-month leave of absence GM offers instead of leaving the company."

Just as he said that, Tom walked up and Danny introduced me. I could tell from their interaction that these two men really seemed to know and respect each other. What a great foundation for Trust!

After the introductions, I asked Tom, "Why did you let Danny take a leave of absence rather than quit outright?"

He answered as a leader who cared, "We have various tools at our disposal to help our people, even those who are considering leaving us. I wasn't certain Danny was sure he really wanted out. So we offered him the program."

When I turned to Danny and jokingly asked, "Well, what do you think? Was it the right move for you?" he responded with a QBQ: "You bet, and now that I'm back, I'm asking, 'How can I contribute?'"

Compare that with the reaction of Vince's boss. Can you feel the difference? Which person would you rather work with? Just imagine what we could do if we had the level of Trust in our organizations and our lives exemplified by Tom and Danny.

The bad news is, if we're being honest with ourselves, most organizations don't have that kind of Trust now. But the good news is that we can. Start with a QBQ such as, "What can I do to build more Trust in all my relationships?"

Let's look at some specific things we can do to create and nurture Trust. I call them the 5 Ts of Trust.

The Five Ts of Trust

1. Time

Our priorities are evident in what we choose to do all day. We have our lists of tasks, our regular chores and our milestones on the way toward meeting goals. Building trustful relationships cannot merely be checked off the list. We have to spend time interacting with, listening to and serving other people. These actions take time.

I remember one day I'd been having a hard time getting through to a vice president, and I was venting to his administrative assistant. "I'm really frustrated, Julie. How do I reach him?" I realized I had said too much, but she surprised me when she lowered her voice and said, "You think that's bad, John? I can't get any time with him either!"

And her desk was right outside his door.

We need to make the time to be available to each other, though I know it's not always the easiest or most convenient thing to do.

I was running late getting to the airport one afternoon. As I packed my bags and hurried around the house to get ready, my daughter Tara, who was nine at the time, was chasing me, trying to get my attention. Finally I stopped, exasperated, and said, "Tara, what do you want?"

"Daddy," she said, "I just wanted to tell you something that happened at school today!"

As I was shutting down my computer, stuffing papers in my briefcase and trying to jot down some notes so I wouldn't lose the thoughts, I said, "Honey, I'm really in a hurry. Can you walk out to the car with me and can you talk real fast?"

She stopped in her tracks. "Never mind," she said as her little head dropped, "I'll wait to tell you when you get home and *you* can listen real slow." Ouch!

Now this is not an excuse, but just so you know, one of the reasons I said what I did is that Tara is our storyteller. If you have one in your house, you know what I mean. When she gets started on a story, we all know she won't be finished for, well, a while. Like all of us, she sometimes starts her stories at inconvenient times. But still, taking time to listen is the right thing to do—and besides, when I listen, I'm building a relationship because I'm building Trust.

Let's suppose that during the next dozen years I continually say to Tara, "Honey, could you please talk faster?" This is what she hears: "I'm not that interested in what you have to say" and "When are you going to change to meet my needs?" Do you think when she's in her twenties she'll still be calling or coming by to share those precious stories with me? I don't think so. And I wouldn't blame her, either. But if I invest time now and send her the message that I am, in fact, *very* interested in what she has to say because she's so important to me, the return will be a lifetime of Tara's stories. If I don't invest the time today, it will be my loss.

If you want to build Trust in your organization, don't be the person who says, "Pete, can you talk real fast? I have to get to a meeting." Trust takes time.

And I'm not talking about the myth of "quality time," either. Of course we want our time together to be quality time, but too often that idea ends up as a rationalization for spending less time together. And that contradicts the fundamental principles of Trust-building. Trust-filled relationships are based on *quantity* time—time invested in each other. Trust is the by-product of the time spent building it.

2. Truth

I was meeting with Sheryl, a prospective client, and I wanted to ask her what I was afraid would seem a "pushy" question. I hesitated, then said, "I'm trying to ask you a question, but I'm not sure how to verbalize it."

She spoke wisdom I've never forgotten, "Why don't you *say* it the way you're *thinking* it?" What a novel idea. I'd better write that down! I've also heard it said this way: "Say what you mean and mean what you say. Just don't be mean when you say it." Either way, that's what positive, constructive communication is all about. Speak the truth.

Many teams could use this concept. I'll always remember one session with a vice president of sales and six regional sales managers sitting around a conference-room table talking about the changes going on in their business. They had some "tough stuff" they needed to announce to the field organization. Suddenly, like a politician caught in a scandal, one of them said, "What kind of a spin can we put on this so the salespeople will buy in?"

That question may begin with the word "What," but it's a bad question. Why put a spin on the message at all? Why not treat people as peers, colleagues and adults, and simply tell them the truth?

Most of us were raised to be honest, but are we really honest? I wonder how often we speak in code and innuendo in our organizations. Do we avoid telling the truth in order to be polite or preserve an illusion? I've heard it said that all lies are self-centered, and I agree. We say we're lying to protect someone else, but we're really protecting ourselves. We're avoiding the pain of speaking the truth.

For example, a manager tells an employee, "You got passed over for the promotion, Ted, because Jim had more years in," instead of speaking directly with Ted about his obvious growth areas. Maybe he doesn't want to hurt Ted's feelings, or does not like conflict or wants to avoid being the bad guy.

Yes, it's difficult to say what is true at times, but truth is the best route. As someone once said, "When I tell the truth I never have to remember later what I said!"

Whom do you trust more, the person who gives you the truth, even if it stings, or the one who works hard to put a spin on it so the sugar-coated pill will go down more easily?

I grow stronger in the long term when I speak—and when I hear—the truth. For a meaningful defense of the power of truth, read Scott Peck's classic, *The Road Less Traveled.*

We could debate the subtleties of honesty, but as a general rule, I've found that where there is more truth, there is more Trust. Let's all work on our truth-telling skills so our relationships can be more filled with Trust.

3. Teaching

Have you heard the axiom, "Knowledge is power?" Some people believe their power is secure only if they keep knowledge to themselves, parceling it out a bit at a time as they deem it necessary. If knowledge is power, they reason, keeping more of it makes them more powerful. I believe giving knowledge away can be the way to growing more powerful. When you give knowledge away, you duplicate yourself. Give others the knowledge they need to succeed and you become a mentor, partner and colleague. And a good team is far more powerful than a greedy individual.

We hear a lot about having mentors and being mentored. What is the foundation of that relationship? Trust. And where does it come from? It stems from the intense and sincere desire to help others become more than they are. I've had many teachers in my life and three I can call mentors: my father, Steve Brown and Jim Strutton. They were always willing to give of themselves to teach me. I want to do that for others.

When I'm willing to teach by sharing my knowledge, gifts and talents, I've demonstrated how much I care about others. I've shown how important they are to me. And, of course, to teach requires another "T" of Trust: time. Teaching builds Trust.

4. Transfer of Authority

When we transfer authority to others, we are saying, "You can do it! Let me know sometime what you did! I trust you!" And Trust breeds Trust.

Now, naturally, as I transfer authority to others, I need to be teaching too, or I may be giving them just enough rope to hang themselves. But generally, when used in balance with all the other "Ts," transferring authority is a great way to build Trust.

Before we talk about how best to transfer authority, let's look at some ways *not* to transfer authority:

Hover. When we truly give others authority, they need not check in with us before they act. We don't say to people, "Come back to me with three options and we'll decide together." We let *them* decide and act.

Too often, managers think they've given someone authority when in fact, they've only put them on a yo-yo, given them some rope and then pulled them right back in. This is not only confusing, but it actually builds distrust instead of Trust. Nothing sends the message, "You are not to be trusted," as much as hovering over someone's shoulder to make sure a project gets done "just right" (translation: my way).

Want to tell someone, "I don't trust you"? Hover.

Meddle. I once asked a middle manager with a wildly profitable and growing firm, "What is the Number One roadblock to getting authority to the grass roots of an organization?" Without a moment's hesitation she spat out this word: meddling! She calls people who meddle, "Meddling Managers." Sounds a bit like hovering, don't you think?

Blame. A poor manager doesn't even get as far as the yo-yo method. He or she holds on to authority, only giving employees responsibility for getting things done. If employees fail, the manager has the authority to punish, withhold rewards or even fire them. It's the carrot-and-stick approach to changing others' behavior, sometimes omitting the carrot. Given enough effective sticks, this approach can work for a while, but it doesn't develop the other person's self-reliance or initiative, and it certainly doesn't build Trust.

Here's the rub: We naturally want to give away accountability and retain authority. Think about it. We say, "Before you take action, check with me for final approval. And by the way, if your plan doesn't work, it's still *your* fault!"

This is the, "I want to make you accountable while I remain in charge!" approach.

How to Transfer Authority

The leadership approach that works best reverses the authority and responsibility. The leader gives away authority to people, who decide how best to get the job done. The responsibility of the leader is to support the team as best she can. If the team fails, the leader has failed to help them succeed.

This leader sees the world differently and says, "I'm accountable but you have the authority, the ability and the power to make the decision and take the action. I will not hover or meddle. If you fail, I will not assign blame. I will ask, 'What can I do to be a more effective leader for you?'"

One of the best illustrations of the proper leadership paradigm takes place, surprisingly enough, on a softball field.

You are the center fielder and the other team is at bat. Your team is ahead by one run in the bottom of the seventh—the last inning of the game. There's a runner on first base. The crack of the bat gets you moving to your left. As you watch the ball fall into the gap between you and the right fielder, you must make a decision. Should you throw the ball to home plate to prevent the tying run from scoring and risk the runner advancing to third? Or should you drill the ball to third and let the run score and the other team tie the game, while holding the batter at second base?

Options. Split-second decisions. Risks. They are all part of the game you love. Finally, the ball is secure in your grip. You turn and ...

... look toward the clubhouse, get the manager's attention and scream, "Boss, Boss, what should I do?"

Of course, I'm kidding. You wouldn't do that. Neither would I.

Here is the key question: When the ball is in your hand and you're preparing to throw, who has the authority to decide what to do in that moment? You! Not the manager. Not another player. Not the team owner. Not the fans. You do. That's true authority, because it's only *after* the action has been taken that the "supervisor" learns what decision was made and implemented.

When People Fail

When we transfer authority, only to learn later that the action someone else has taken produces a negative result, does that mean we have transferred too much authority? Let's learn from a story that sounds unbelievable but is true nonetheless.

At a restaurant I know well, a server spilled red wine on a man's suit. The server apologized profusely. She told him to bring her the receipt for dry cleaning the suit, and he would be reimbursed. A week later he returned without a dry-cleaning bill. The stain wouldn't come out, he told her. She apologized again, and made a decision in the moment—a decision that required Courage, I might add. She told him to go buy a new suit and her company would cover it.

To her surprise, he was back within the hour with an Armani suit. Are you ready for this? $1,200. Was he taking advantage of her? Maybe. Or maybe it really was the replacement cost of his other suit. Either way, when he handed her the bill, she was shaking with fear.

Moments later, she handed her general manager the clothing store receipt. The manager stared at it for a moment and then calmly asked the server how she would handle the situation differently in the future. That's good coaching. The manager knew a teachable moment when she saw one. After a brief discussion, she reached for the company checkbook and wrote the patron a check for $1,200. She handed it to the server and said simply, "Would you please give him this along with our invitation to return with a guest and have dinner on us?" And that was that.

Someone hearing this for the first time would possibly want to attack the customer with the appetite for expensive suits. Or we might say, "That's one server who didn't deserve to be 'empowered!'" Or, "Why didn't they fire her for her error in judgment?"

But I believe the server did the right thing—except, of course, that she did not give the customer a parameter. Was that a tactical error? Probably. But at the moment she brought the manager the receipt, it was a non-issue.

Let's look at the questions the manager could have asked: "Why did you do something so stupid?" "When will you learn?" "Who does the customer think he is, anyway?" But she didn't ask these questions. Instead, she had the amazing discipline simply to write the check and support the server! That's what impresses me. After this experience, how do you think the server felt about the general manager?

The food-service industry suffers from about 100 percent turnover. What does that cost? More than can ever be calculated in hard numbers. A lot more than $1,200. By backing up the server in her promise to the customer, the manager built an immeasurable amount of Trust.

Transfer Authority—Transfer Trust

Now, here's a key guideline to remember when transferring authority: Only give authority to the point the other person remains accountable. In other words, at the moment people refuse to accept Personal Accountability for their actions and start engaging in Blame, Procrastination or Victim Thinking, do *not* transfer any more authority.

The natural consequence of choosing the wrong path should be the loss of additional authority. But in our example, the server showed remorse and demonstrated she was accountable. She didn't accuse the customer of tripping her, complain about how busy she was or blame the lack of sleep as the real culprit. She is a person worth keeping!

Trust cannot be bought, hired or trained. It comes only from experiences such as the one above. Think of the shame, the humiliation, the degradation the manager could have bestowed upon the server. Instead, she asked better questions and made better choices. She is a leader, and she has a leader working alongside her, too!

Transferring authority says, "I trust you." The better you are at it, the more Trust there will be in your relationships and your organization.

5. Talking

By talking, I mean speaking directly to others as opposed to speaking behind their backs. Do you know what "triangling" is? Triangling takes place when person A is upset with person B, but instead talks to person C about the issue. Person C says, "I don't like person B either. I don't even know how B stays employed here." We've all seen it—and done it—haven't we?

Sometimes the scenario seems minor: two grown siblings talking casually about Mother or team members moving naturally into an area of discussion that really should involve everyone on the team. But too often, one person is avoiding accountability and risk by venting to a third party without the target party present. More often than not, this accomplishes nothing and actually makes things worse. We can avoid these consequences by talking directly to the person with whom we have an issue.

I have a client named Dan, the president of a large travel organization. He told me that when he first arrived, "Frank" would come into his office, shut the door and begin talking about "Joe"—triangling. But Dan had a great way of responding.

Dan would interrupt Frank mid-sentence and say, "Excuse me!"

Then he'd pick up his phone, dial Joe's extension and say, "Hey Joe, would you please come to my office? Frank wants to speak to you."

Of course, Frank would begin to spit and sputter about not wanting to talk directly to Joe. Dan would reply very seriously, "Pardon me, I thought you had a problem that needed to be solved. If you don't, neither Joe nor I, nor this organization, have time for this!"

"Tell me again," I asked Dan. "How long have you been doing this?"

"About three years," he responded.

"And how have people responded to this approach?"

With a twinkle in his eye, he said, "Well, John, they don't come to me anymore!"

Good for Dan. No leader should begin or participate in a triangle. Even when triangling seems innocent enough, it breeds fragmentation in any group. I've seen this happen over and over again. If you have a problem with someone, the absolute best way to deal with it, and the only accountable thing to do, is to talk to that person directly. The benefits are tremendous: stronger communication, better problem solving, more Trust.

Politically Speaking

A close cousin to triangling is organizational politics. Talk about a productivity killer! Let's define politics as when the "who" is more important than the "what." That means we're more concerned with the *source* of an idea than with the idea itself.

"What? A software developer on third floor discovered the cure for the common cold? Well, I don't believe it'll ever work!"

But let's say the president discovered the cure. Then people would more likely say, "Oh, what a terrific idea!"

Duane Halverson, executive vice president and COO of Land 'O Lakes, told me the best people in that organization simply focus on doing the job and don't get drawn into politics. It goes without saying we should all do the same.

An executive vice president of a large insurance group once expressed a frustration to me. "John, I just don't get it. My staff and I sit in a meeting, the heads nod up and down and we all agree to a plan. Then a day later, through a circuitous route, I find out someone doesn't think the plan will work! Why don't people speak up?"

Obviously, there's a QBQ he could be asking, but the bottom line is still politics and triangling. His staff would express their concerns to someone else (triangling) but not to the boss (politics).

Another corporate client shared with me off the record that everybody takes the temperature of the president before presenting an idea. The general consensus is this: Stay away from him on Monday, approach him on Friday. What happens Tuesday through Thursday? No sharing of ideas? No raising of issues? This is a waste, don't you think, to have adults maneuvering and planning their lives around the mood of one person? Once again, politics.

Politics and triangling are all part of the same game: putting on masks, not speaking plainly, protecting the feelings of one individual rather than promoting the welfare of the entire organization—or simply protecting ourselves. We can do better.

Eliminating triangling and politics builds major Trust. By talking directly to each other, we send messages of respect, camaraderie, shared commitment and maturity. People thrive, teams work, business grows. Become vigilant about avoiding triangling and politics, and you'll see a real difference.

Making Trust Personal

Here's a quick review of some ideas that build Trust. Remember, Trust is building another's confidence in me through what I say and do. Five ways to do this:

1. Give time.

2. Speak truth.

3. Teach.

4. Transfer authority.

5. Talk directly.

Here are some questions to help bring the Pillar of Trust to life. Take a few minutes right now to answer these.

1. What behaviors do I engage in that reduce the Trust in my relationships?

2. How can I eliminate those actions today and replace them with better ones?

3. In what relationship do I want to build more Trust?

4. Of the five Ts of Trust, where am I strong and where do I need to improve today?

Pillar Principle Eight: Clarity

Her name was Heather and she was a bundle of energy, enthusiasm and excitement as she rushed up to me and asked a very strange question, "Are you John Miller?"

"Ah, well, weren't you in the audience?" I had just finished a keynote address in a Houston hotel ballroom, and her question seemed a bit out of place.

"No," she told me, "I was out in the hallway. I'm here for another meeting but I listened to part of your talk through a crack in the door." She went on to tell me the QBQ had really caught her attention and she took notes standing outside the ballroom. I thanked her for her kind words and encouraged her to apply the QBQ.

Then, out of the blue she said with great conviction, "I'm a speaker too, you know!"

"What do you mean?" I asked. She explained that she loves to get up in front of groups to inspire and teach. She's involved in an organization that holds lots of meetings so she has a natural venue for using her skills, gifts and talents.

I was very impressed. Still, in spite of her poise and professionalism, her youthfulness made me curious. I took a risk and asked her age. She floored me. "Sixteen!"

I don't know about you, but I didn't possess that kind of Clarity at 16. Did you? Do we have it even now?

The Pillar of Clarity involves more than knowing where we want to go and more than having a goal. It also involves knowing who we are and why we want to get there. And, because Clarity guides us in the moment-to-moment decisions we make, this Pillar Principle is indispensable to the journey of Personal Accountability.

Clarity is a powerful ally in helping us accomplish more for ourselves and our organizations. Clarity will help us formulate the QBQs that are essential for good decisions. That's why Clarity needs to be sought out, developed and continually renewed.

The Search for Clarity

Let's think of Clarity this way:

Clearly defining the Why, What and How of my life.

Said differently, Clarity encompasses my mission, vision and the principles I value. Let's explore each of these areas separately as we search for the answer to the QBQ, "What can I do to create Clarity in my life?"

I. Mission: Why do I exist?

For Clarity, we must have a mission, or purpose. Here's the definition we'll use:

Mission: the "Why" of my life

Sometimes we get so focused on our accomplishments—the awards we've won, the money we've made, the status we've achieved—that we simply forget *why* we're here.

Craig Pixley is a friend and a business associate. He loves to sell and service his customers. That's where his heart is, but we all can get off track. In his work for Northwestern Incentive Services, Craig often travels to beautiful places with client groups. While there, he spends time with customers, making sure their needs are met. This is the "service after the sell." One time he found himself in Hawaii for several days hosting a major corporate account.

Craig was escorting four executives to the golf course for a 6 a.m. tee time. The course was a fair distance from the resort and there was a chilly mist in the air. Craig was feeling a bit tired and cold. By the time he delivered the foursome to their appointed spot, well equipped and apparently very happy, he was anxious to get back to his room for a hot shower.

Unfortunately, one of the men had another idea.

"I sure could use a cup of strong, hot Hawaiian coffee!" he said. Then he turned to a friend. "How about you, Tom?" Tom quickly agreed and the other two chimed in their affirmations. They all stared at Craig, but before he could respond, Tom thought of something else. He said to Craig, smiling yet serious, "And what I'd really like is one of those huge cinnamon buns they have back at the restaurant!"

The "Me toos" came fast and furious.

What was Craig to say? "Right away, gentlemen. I'd love to help you out!" All the while, he was thinking, I don't believe this is happening!

Craig dutifully headed off in a golf cart down the cold, wet path, with the damp air blowing in his face and the goose bumps on his arms growing larger by the minute. With each thought, the drive seemed longer: I can't believe I'm doing this. I sold them this trip and I've gone the extra mile to help them. I'm 45 years old and I deserve better. When is someone going to do something for me? Why do I get stuck with the coffee addicts? Who do they think they are to send me, Craig Pixley, for coffee and rolls; that's certainly not my ... .

As his mind was racing, understandably, with those thoughts, Jacob came to mind. Remember Jacob Miller from the Rock Bottom Brewery Restaurant, who made it his own personal mission to get me a Diet Coke? Craig knows that story. Right then and there, Craig remembered Jacob and had a profound thought: This *is* why I exist! Not to run for coffee and cinnamon buns, necessarily, but, like Jacob, to make sure the customers have exactly what they want. This is why I'm here. This is my purpose.

With the change in his thinking came a change in his feelings, and suddenly it wasn't all that cold after all. In fact, he started to notice what a beautiful Hawaiian day it was, and how happy he was to be doing his job. All from a simple dose of considering the first step of Clarity: *mission.*

Getting clear on the "Why" of our life, our mission, puts things in a better light and makes the drudgeries easier to live with. Sometimes this kind of focus takes a lifetime. Sometimes it happens in a heartbeat.

An Unexpected Lesson

At 6 o'clock one morning, I was driving on an icy road, heading to my health club for a racquetball match. I had just rolled out of bed and my eyes were a bit fuzzy. I was regretting my resolution to stay in shape, when, suddenly, I saw up ahead what looked like a big, black hole, centered in my field of vision. It was darker than the morning darkness and at first I thought it was some combination of the mist and snow that hung in the air.

I slowed. It was a car, overturned on the center median. I quickly pulled over. No other cars were coming from either direction. I bolted to the driver's side, looked in, and found a man hanging upside down by his seat belt. The window had shattered, and glass was everywhere. "Are you all right?" I asked.

"Yeah, I think I am," he said.

"How long have you been here?"

"Just happened a minute ago," he replied in a groggy tone. Afraid to move him myself, I said, "Don't move while I get my cell phone!" I ran over to my car, and as I reached in for my phone I heard a car door shut. Good, some help has arrived, I thought. As I backed out of my car and turned, I bumped right into a man in his 30s. "Oh, excuse me," I offered, not knowing where he had come from.

"I guess I'm OK," he said. Then I realized he was the man who moments earlier had been hanging upside-down in his car.

"Great," I said, feeling relieved. "Let's call 911 anyway!"

He agreed but asked, "Can I use your phone first?" I quickly handed it to him as I stepped a few feet away into the darkness. While watching the Minnesota sunrise, I heard some beautiful words. "Hi, Dear … . Yeah, I'm gonna be a little late getting home this morning. No problems, my shift was fine. I'm kind of tired, though." Then there was a pause followed by, "Honey, have I told you lately how much I love you?"

I experienced that moment many years ago and now, for both his sake and mine, I'm glad it happened. I'm not happy that he totalled his car, but since there were no injuries, if that rollover helped him define more clearly what was meaningful for him and why he exists, it was worthwhile. His words added value to my life, too. Sometimes, as we pursue our dreams we sacrifice the very thing—or person—whose loss would hurt us most. The picture of that man and his upside-down car has stayed with me, as has the memory of what he said to his wife.

Life has a way of handing us moments and images that stick with us and remind us of our "Why."

The Mission Statement

Most people have not written a personal mission statement, but it's the first step toward practicing the Pillar Principle of Clarity. When I have clarified my own mission statement, I am much better able to make the consistent decisions that characterize Personal Accountability.

A mission is not a picture, goal or vision. It is *not* about being the biggest, the best or the boldest. It's the "Why" behind what we do each day. It's our purpose for being here. Before writing your mission statement, you may want to consider these guidelines for creating one that works:

1. Answer a critical question.

Have you asked, and answered, the key question, "Why do I exist?" Said differently, "How can I define my purpose?"

My mission statement articulates the purpose of my existence. I need to make sure it answers these questions—nothing more, nothing less.

Remember, the answers are in the questions—always.

2. Use twelve words or fewer.

When it comes to an effective mission statement, less is more. We are really forced to think when we limit our mission to a dozen words max, not even a baker's dozen. As a general rule, the shorter the mission statement, the clearer and more powerful. And, let's face it, if we can't remember our mission, it's of no value.

I worked on this with a senior management team in the lumber and home building products business. They had produced a mission statement a year or two earlier which, not atypically, was a full page long and did not serve them well. I encouraged the managers to think about how they could get it down to 12 or fewer words. After some effort, they came up with, "Helping People Build Their Dreams." Now that's a mission, don't you think? Concise enough to commit to memory and meaningful enough to commit to!

3. Make the mission timeless.

A good mission statement never wears out. We keep it from becoming dated by *not* referring to products, professions or time frames. My mission is this: "Helping People Ask the Question Behind the Question." My purpose for existence is *not* to be a great speaker getting lots of applause, conquering the world and earning tons of money with X number of annual engagements by a certain year. My mission is focused on *why* I exist, and it is something I can accomplish for years to come, in lots of ways.

As a parent, speaker, consultant and author, I can help people ask the QBQ. I can accomplish this through audio cassettes, CDs, the ChartHouse Learning film, this book. I can still fulfill my purpose, whether I am a United States Congressman, a college professor or a missionary. Since my mission is not tied to one delivery vehicle, I have focus, flexibility and freedom. A mission statement should focus on just that: the mission.

4. Base your mission on the Pillar of Service.

Late one evening, I met a woman in Las Vegas who had a clear mission. Yet I doubt it served her well. I was going down in the elevator at Caesar's Palace, where I had delivered a talk. I needed to catch the "red eye" back to Chicago. The elevator stopped on the seventh floor and a tired, discouraged-looking woman stepped in. I noticed she was clutching a $20 bill in one hand.

She took her other hand and stretched the bill before her, staring down at it intensely. I didn't say a word. Then she slowly lifted her head, looked me, a total stranger, in the eye and said grimly, "I'm gonna play 'til I lose this!"

An effective mission statement needs to have the right focus. And that focus is, "You first, me second." If in any way a mission communicates, "My needs before yours," "Look out for Number One" or "I deserve and am entitled," the mission is not a sound one. I am amazed at the number of corporate management teams—and individuals—who believe "Profit first, then we'll serve!"

People and groups of people who prosper for the long haul *always* focus on serving others. They practice the Pillar Principle of Service, which, in this sense, is more than a value; it functions as a natural law and you break it at your own peril.

If we defy the natural law of gravity, we're bound to take a fall. The same is true if we break the natural Law of Service: "Prosperity is in direct proportion to the quality and quantity of service rendered." I learned that principle from Steve Brown. Make sure your mission statement is based on the Pillar of Service.

5. Connect your mission with the principles you value.

My mission, "Helping People Ask the Question Behind the Question," has one word in it that connects it with a key principle I value: I can only change me. To better communicate this principle, I purposely chose to use the word "people" in my purpose statement rather than the word "others," so my statement would communicate that it is not just others who need the QBQ. "Helping Others ... " would essentially say, "I don't need the QBQ but you sure do!" In my mind, "People" includes me. Choose each word carefully as you craft your mission statement and make sure it connects with the principles *you* value.

A quick review of our mission statement guidelines:

1. Answer the question, "Why do I exist?"
2. Use 12 words or fewer.
3. Make the mission timeless.
4. Base it on the Pillar of Service.
5. Connect your mission with the principles you value.

If your mission statement follows these five guidelines, you'll be well on your way to greater Clarity in your life. While these guidelines are fresh in your mind, take a few minutes, and on a separate piece of paper, and try writing your own personal mission statement. Don't be too frustrated if it doesn't seem finished the first time. This process takes some real thought and effort. But defining your own mission is well worth doing even if you don't finalize it on the first try, because the thought process itself will move you a long way toward Clarity.

II. Vision: What do I want to become?

Vision is the second step in our search for Clarity. Let's define vision as this:

Vision: What I choose to become; a picture of what I plan to be

My dad, serving as Cornell's wrestling coach for so many years, introduced me to many special people. One of them was Professor Dan.

Professor Dan was probably the wrestling team's greatest fan. He attended every meet, cheering from the stands for each wrestler. He always had a smile for us, and was generous with comments such as, "Well, don't you look great today! What a beautiful, bright shirt you have on. That color blue is perfect for you." Yes, Dan possessed a positive attitude, a zest for life—and an outlook on his world that was well, unique.

He had a crazy way of exercising. He'd tether himself to a pole in the center of his back yard with a rope tied loosely around his waist. Then he would run in circles. Can you picture that? Actually, it's not really all that crazy when you realize that Professor Dan is blind.

It happened in the Korean War and at that point he had a choice, as we all do. He could ask the Victim's IQ, "Why did this happen to me?" or the Procrastinator's IQ, "When is someone going to take care of me?" Instead, he chose the path of Personal Accountability by asking, "What can I do to become something more than I am today?"

In spite of his "disability," Dan had a strong vision for what he wanted to become, and that vision led him to Cornell where he became a world-renowned professor of agriculture. And the wrestling team's Number One fan.

Whatever future you see for yourself, having a clear vision of it is key to your success. As J. C. Penney once said (paraphrased), "Show me a stock clerk with a goal and I'll show you a person who will conquer the world, but show me a person with no goals and I'll show you a stock clerk!"

A Plan of Action for Defining My Vision

There's nothing like a good, practical plan to help us accomplish our task. Here are nine guidelines on how to create a vision.

1. Focus on one area of my life.

We are integrated beings. That is, the various aspects of our lives really cannot be isolated from each other. We aren't separate financial persons, social persons, professional persons, spiritual persons and family persons. Instead, our "persons" are mixed into the same melting pot.

This integration is evident when a problem in one area of my life affects the other areas. A conflict in my professional life affects my home life. Relational struggles in my family can have a spiritual impact. Challenges with my finances may diminish my ability to achieve Excellence in my profession.

Because I am a whole, integrated person, sometimes it's hard to focus on just one area, but that's the first step in creating a powerful vision. The up-side of this is that my successes in one area positively affect other areas. The key is to choose an area, whether financial, spiritual, physical, mental, emotional or professional, and define my vision.

2. Honestly assess where I am today.

Visualize with me: Today I will blindfold you in downtown Patterson, New Jersey, put you in a vehicle and drive for half a day with no stops. Then I'll transfer you to a boat for a day, and you will feel the water beneath the vessel. Don't worry, you'll be well fed. Finally, I will take you for a plane ride. The plane sounds like an older model prop plane, but at least the engine doesn't quit. Finally, I'll escort you from the plane and remove the kerchief from your eyes.

Question: Do you believe with all your heart that you could return to the starting point of beautiful Patterson, New Jersey?

Any of us could—given enough time and resources. But when that blindfold comes off, what is the very first thing you will need to know? That's right, where you are! That's the way it is in the visioning process. If I don't know where I am, I'm lost.

I can only determine where I am in this process by ruthlessly taking inventory of my skills, gifts and talents, my current thoughts, emotions and practices. Only then, from the beginning, can I take the first step every journey requires. I need to evaluate honestly where I am today in terms of my strengths and growth areas (translation: weaknesses).

3. Define my actual vision.

This step in our plan of action is the crux of the entire process, and it became more personal on a family trip to Phoenix. During that vacation, Karen and I decided to take a day and do the unthinkable with four kids under the age of 14: Drive five hours up to the Grand Canyon and five hours back in the same day.

Halfway back to our Scottsdale hotel, after many hours in the car, Tara, who bores easily like her dad, asked, "Mom, do we have a United States map in the car?"

Karen told her she was sorry but we didn't. Pondering her request, I said, "Honey, why would you want a map of the whole country?"

With despair in her voice, she responded, "Oh, I just wanted to see where I *could be* right now compared with where I am!"

That's a healthy desire. If I want to move from where I am right now, I need to set my sights on where I want to go! I just have to make sure my sights are set on the goal that is right for me, or else I may get lost.

I was visiting good friends in Rochester, Minnesota, one New Year's Eve. After dinner, I headed out alone for a half-hour walk. It was dark and a thick fog had rolled in.

Since I was in an unfamiliar neighborhood, I chose as a landmark a water tower with a bright red light on top about a block from my friends' home. Feeling confident this beacon would guide me, I headed out into the abyss.

After about 15 minutes, having never lost sight of the red light, I turned around and headed home. Another 15 minutes passed, though, then 30, and I was still in unfamiliar territory.

Even when I encountered a six-foot-wide creek that hadn't been there before, I was confident of my landmark. With my eye on the goal, I crossed the creek and climbed a chain link fence, tearing my jeans. Then I clamored up a slippery slope of rocks, mud and snow.

"Finally, I'm here!" I crowed to myself. Yes, I had arrived at the red light. One problem: It was the *wrong* red light. This one sat atop a radio station tower—fully four miles from my starting point! My clothes were torn, wet and muddy and I was cold. I was also totally off course (a male euphemism for "lost").

Why? My sights had been set on the wrong goal.

As I emerged from the woods, stealthily moving through peoples' backyards, I spied a man just climbing into his car with his daughter. I summoned some Courage, dashed from the shadows and virtually accosted them to ask for help. Once the initial shock wore off, my Good Samaritan took me back to the red light on the water tower, and from there we found my friends' home.

Be careful what you set your sights on. Only you can decide which beacon to follow, which vision is best for you.

Let me share with you the criteria for a solid vision. They follow the acrostic, V-I-S-I-O-N. All visions are:

V - Valid in purpose. Every vision must have a "why." That means my vision needs to be in line with my mission. One way to check for this is to imagine myself sometime in the future, after I've realized my vision. If I have stayed true to my mission, then my vision and mission are probably in line with each other. On the other hand, if I have achieved my vision but veered off course from my mission along the way, I've been pursuing the wrong vision.

Major Kevin Little of the U.S. Air Force helped me understand the power of purpose. Of the aircraft crashes in the military, he told me, fully 85 percent can be traced to a common cause: A person in the manufacturing or maintenance process did not understand the "Why" of his or her job. The inability of these people to see themselves and their tasks as crucial can be deadly for pilots. In a much different sense, of course, not understanding the "Why" behind my activities can be deadly to my vision. My vision must be grounded in the "Why," my mission.

I - Imagined vividly. I must be able to see my vision in my mind. This is so simple, yet so profound. I must own my vision. So often, people try to live out their lives for someone else: a son for a father, a husband for a wife, an employee for a manager. This will not work. Ownership comes only from creating the goal for myself. I own that which I create and can see in my mind's eye.

Earl Nightingale, the great teacher of self development concepts, compared the human brain with a movie theater's wide screen. I can decide what gets projected onto my screen. I can vividly imagine on that screen whatever I choose, putting it on pause to examine it more carefully whenever I choose. This is why we've talked so much about putting our thoughts on hold and deliberately choosing QBQs instead of IQs in the pressure of the moment. What I can imagine I am more likely to become. If I can't envision it, the dream surely will never be brought to reality.

I'll never forget the night in 1992 that I sat on the couch in my robe close to midnight watching a video of Zig Ziglar presenting to a large audience. I saw the fun he was having. The crowd was laughing and learning at the same time. Zig was making a difference in people's lives. I had worked with groups for seven years primarily as a facilitator, but not as a keynote speaker.

Alone, I pointed at the TV and said these words out loud: "That's what I want to do! That's what I want to be!" I don't claim to be Zig, but I do claim to have seen my vision first in my head. Later, the vision became reality.

S - Seen as realistic. I must believe my vision is possible. Realism has nothing to do with the scope of the vision. The personal vision I'm trying to achieve can be large or small. What matters is only whether *I* believe I can do it. If I do, then it is realistic. Remember, those around us may think it impossible, but that doesn't matter. Many a goal has been killed while still in the seed stage because we shared it with someone who stomped it out with words such as, "You'll never do it!" "Why would you want to do that?" and "When are you going to get a real job, anyway?"

One woman, a dear friend, told me how at the age of 10, while watching Chad Everett on the old TV show "Medical Center," she proudly told her mom, "I'm going to be a doctor!" But her mother responded, "That takes a lot of schooling and you may not have the grades." Partly because of her mom's discouraging words, my friend became a nurse instead, which is fine of course, but she's always wondered whether she had the "stuff" to make it as a doctor.

It is not easy to ignore the opinions of those closest to us, but the reality is that sometimes we must. History is full of examples of "impossible" dreams that came true with incredible success. If everyone says no, but you can still see it clearly in your mind, go for it. It's a realistic vision to the one who counts: *you*.

I - Immersed in feedback. We must find out how we're doing. If I just want to "lose some weight," it'll be tough. But if I have specific targets to shoot for, I can get some valuable information along the way. When I look past my toes to the dial on the scale, I'll either say, "Wow, I'm ahead of plan! Good for me!" or I'll know I need to make some adjustments to realize my vision.

When a space shuttle blasts off, how many adjustments do you think NASA's computers make to keep it on course? More than we can count. I, too, need input to help me stay on track. As noted in the chapter on Excellence, a coach can help me tremendously in this area. No matter how I get feedback, as I move toward my vision, I need to seek the input that can guide me.

O - Overtly timed. I've heard it said that, "Goals are dreams with deadlines," and I believe that's true. Without a deadline, the energy, resources and personal drive required to accomplish my vision don't come together. Like a diamond, my goals need pressure to become a reality. In this case, that pressure is a deadline. Until I give my vision a deadline, it is just something I may do someday. And then Procrastination, the Friend of Failure, arrives on my doorstep and I pay the price in missed opportunities and lost progress.

A deadline brings urgency. I believe successful people live lives of urgency tempered with mature patience. They understand that time is required to grow seeds and to reap a harvest. They also understand that today's action is to plant the seed. Action requires energy, which is based on urgency—which comes from deadlines. Set some today!

N - Nurtures learning. Our goal must motivate us to learn, change and grow. A vision that does not create in us a positive tension that pulls us forward, is not a worthwhile vision. There's a correlation between this guideline and the Pillar of Excellence. If you remember, we defined Excellence as, *"Celebrating the achievement of a new level of performance while setting my sights beyond."*

Our vision should pull us, as a child pulls a toy around on a string, away from where we are today and toward where our sights are set, that is, what we plan to be.

When I met Jerry Knight, now the CFO of Fingerhut Companies, Inc., he was the CFO of Toro, the maker of lawn mowers, snow blowers and other home and industrial products. Jerry went to his staff one day in 1995 (when the Internet was relatively new to business) and told them he wanted to learn to "surf the Net." Someone on his team said, "Jerry, you've had a great career with G.E., Black and Decker and Pillsbury and now you're our CFO. Why would you want to waste your time learning about the Internet?"

Jerry's response is a classic. He told his team, "So I can stay up with the eight-year-old who lives next door!"

Jerry is a perfect example of someone who continually establishes a vision that nurtures the Pillar of Learning. Make sure your vision nurtures Learning in you too, and requires you to stretch beyond where you are today.

Those are the six criteria for a powerful vision, and defining the vision is Step 3 in our plan of action. Let's quickly review them.

V-I-S-I-O-N:

V - Valid in purpose
I - Imagined vividly
S - Seen as realistic
I - Immersed in feedback
O - Overtly timed
N - Nurtures learning

Now, with our six criteria in place for setting our sights on where we want to go, we return to our plan of action.

4. Identify the tools I need to get from here to there.

In order to get from where I am to where I want to be, what resources (people, knowledge, skills) do I need? List them on paper. Resources may include groups, mentors, dollars, training, physical resources and any number of other things.

For example, when I first entered the business of professional speaking, I quickly discovered I needed an information kit, including a preview video, audio tapes and a folder explaining my ideas and my background. But I didn't know anything about creating those tools, so I found people with the appropriate expertise to create them for me.

What is required for you to achieve your vision? Identify those tools and start building the toolkit you need.

One cannot scale a mountain, win a battle or swim a sea without the right tools. True? Well, sometimes. As we build that tool kit, if we also will keep the Pillar of Creativity in mind, we will continue to ask the QBQ, "What can I do right now, right here to accomplish my vision with the resources I already have?" In seeking to acquire tools, let's remember often the best resource we have is our own Creativity.

5. Identify potential roadblocks.

I need to search out and name possible barriers to my vision. Otherwise, I can be blind-sided by obstacles I could have foreseen. In 1995, I placed a business card under the glass on my desk (the same glass Michael crashed through two years later), and left it there for a year. I looked at it often. It wasn't until 1996 that I began using e-mail for the first time. E-mail was fun and different, and I collected "pen" pals quickly.

One day, to my surprise, I glanced at the card beneath the glass, and guess what I saw? That's right, an e-mail address. I had never seen it before. Why did I suddenly notice it? My mind had been opened by the mere fact that I now had my own e-mail address.

Did you see a forest green, late model Ford Taurus with a luggage rack on the highway today? No? You would have seen half a dozen if you'd bought one yesterday.

This is exactly how it is with potential pitfalls to our plan. Just as I didn't notice the e-mail address, and you probably don't notice the green Taurus, we often are blindsided by potential pitfalls. We can live for months—or years—completely oblivious to them. Yet unless we stop to consider what could possibly go wrong, these blind spots can be our undoing.

Ask yourself, "What might go wrong? What's the worst-case scenario? What surprises might I encounter?" Think about potential pitfalls and plan for them now, and you'll be ready should they come.

6. Create a "Plan B."

Steps 1 through 4 above help me create my plan of attack, "Plan A." Now I need to put together a Plan B, based on the potential pitfalls I identified in Step 5.

By the time each space shuttle crew flies, the pilots have spent literally thousands of hours in flight simulators, practicing "what if" scenarios. In the same way, I need a fall-back position. This keeps me agile, flexible, ready to change and adapt on a moment's notice. What is your Plan B?

7. Be vigilant about my time and energy.

I've learned I need to identify and guard against things that will steal my finite resources of time and energy. Do you like to watch TV, stroll the mall, read a good novel, putter in the garage? Sure, we all do some of these things, and there's nothing inherently wrong with them. However, remember this: *Unseized time will always gravitate to our weaknesses.*

We must be vigilant and stand our guard.

As my mentor Steve Brown says, people who don't attain their vision are more focused on "pleasing activities" than on engaging in "pleasing results." It's certainly fun to have fun, but I need to make sure I am seizing the time and energy needed to engage in those activities that produce pleasing results—the ones that contribute to my vision.

8. Study achievers around me.

Think of those who have already accomplished what you wish to accomplish and learn from their achievements. When we think of learning, we often think of books, but emulating successful people also is powerful. I will tell you passionately that I've learned much more from the three mentors in life—my father, Steve Brown and Jim Strutton—than I could ever gain through written words.

Do you have mentors? I hope so. Mine have been invaluable as I strive to live my mission and achieve my vision. If you don't have mentors, you can still find great value, wisdom and inspiration in studying people who've accomplished what you want to accomplish and learning from their success.

9. Take the leap of faith.

Step out and take a risk! Take action. Maybe you've heard it said, "When you get to the end of your rope, tie a knot and hang on!" What we're talking about here is applying faith, which translates into getting to the end of our rope and *letting go*. If I say I believe in my plan of action, then I must act on that stated belief or I'll never attain my vision. Faith is belief applied. Try letting go. Great things just might happen.

Leaps of faith take Courage, so you might want to take another look at the Pillar of Courage. But remember that nothing is achieved without action, so go to the edge and take the leap. Belief without action is worthless.

Let's review the nine steps for creating a powerful vision. Following these steps will help me define and attain my own personal vision and move me another step closer to the Pillar of Clarity.

1. Focus on one area of my life.
2. Honestly assess where I am today.
3. Define my actual vision. (Use the V-I-S-I-O-N criteria.)
4. Identify the tools I need to get from here to there.
5. Identify potential roadblocks.
6. Have a "Plan B."
7. Be vigilant about my time and energy.
8. Study achievers around me.
9. Take the leap of faith.

III. Values: How will I make choices?

The third step toward Clarity is values. We hear a lot of talk about values these days, but what are they?

Let's define the term as follows:

Values: Principles I hold in high esteem, which guide my decision making

Values are the "how" because they are the principles that guide me. They are the parameters that keep me on track. This, of course, assumes I'm living in accordance with them, and that's one of the challenges we struggle with from day to day.

We'll get deeper into the whole subject of living in accordance with our values when we study the Pillar Principle of Integrity in the next chapter. But in order to live by them, we first have to define them for ourselves. So for now, let's simply work on providing an answer to the QBQ, "How can I define the principles that will guide my decisions?"

In reality, this entire book is about defining values, or choosing the principles that will guide my life. I can certainly use any or all of the Pillar Principles to direct me. But before I do, I need to understand the purpose of values: Values allow me, in the moment, to make better choices.

Just as the QBQ is a tool that enables me to think and act accountably, the principles I use as criteria for making decisions each moment of the day, shape not only my behaviors and practices, but my character.

Do you remember the budget system Karen and I use for our kids presented in the Pillar of Creativity? Is its core purpose to teach our children how to handle money? No, that is a benefit. What the budget system really does is help young people learn what many grown-ups struggle with daily: how to make better decisions—decisions that lead to greater prosperity in all areas of their lives.

Two Different Values

Karen and I were on our way to a day of great skiing in the Little Belt Mountains of Montana, when I lost my wallet. We had stopped to help out at an accident scene (again, no serious injuries), and while out of the car, my wallet, packed with good stuff, fell out into the snowy ditch. When I realized it was gone, panic struck. My money, license, credit cards—gone.

I returned home later that day in great despair to find that a man had dropped it off at my house in Great Falls, fully 50 miles from the accident site! And all the good stuff was still there. What a relief. And what a great thing he did in returning it.

A decade later, I was on my way home from the grocery store on a perfect Minnesota summer day. I suddenly realized I had left two 24-packs of Diet Coke, my favorite, in the bottom rack of the cart back in the store's parking lot. From the time I had driven away, it took me maybe eight minutes total to get back to the cart. The Coke was gone. I checked inside at the customer service desk. Nope. It was gone forever.

Key question: What makes one person drive 50 miles out of the way to return a wallet and another steal 48 cans of warm soda? Answer: values—the principles we commit to that shape our lives each day, the values demonstrated in our choices and our actions.

I make decisions all day, every day (and you do, too) based on the options before me and their corresponding consequences. There are consequences, for example, if I don't pay my taxes. And there are consequences if I don't make it to my children's soccer games: less Trust in my relationships with my kids—and my wife, as she wears herself out chauffeuring.

In every case, I decide. If I'm feeling "All stressed up and nowhere to go," it's the result of my own choices. If I'm spending too much time at work and too little with my family, that's my choice. My values affect my choices all day long. Like a rudder on a ship, they guide me. As I look at my options I'll be happier when I make better choices—those that are in line with my mission, vision and values.

What Values Are Not

Many people confuse values with skills. For example, coaching is a skill, *not* a value. When I decide as a coach to engage in Service, however, I'm demonstrating a principle I value.

Listening is *not* a value; it's another skill. But Trust is a principle I can value and it can lead me to work at understanding others better, which entails listening.

Leadership is *not* a value, management techniques are *not* values, being the best supervisor in the plant is *not* a value. But Learning is a principle a leader values and can ascribe to and it leads to enhanced skills in many areas.

Distinguishing between skills and values is not a science, but as we strive to further define our values, we need to choose principles that serve as a rudder for the decisions we make each day.

Ask yourself: What are the principles I believe in? What principles am I willing to go to the mat for? (In the next chapter, we'll talk about one person who did just that—literally.) Certainly the Pillars represent several possibilities. Superman's guiding values are "Truth, Justice, and the American Way." We all find our own, and they may change as we move from one phase of our lives to the next. But making sure we have a well-defined idea of what we stand for is a critical component of Clarity.

Clarity Revisited

We've looked now at the three essential elements of Clarity: mission, vision and values. We've explored several practical ideas for creating Clarity, which we described this way:

Clearly defining the Why, What and How of my life

Our mission may be timeless, but visions can and do change. Principles never change, of course, but we may choose to be guided by different principles at different times in our lives. Continually asking the QBQ, "What actions can I take today to create Clarity in my life?" is an excellent way to help us stay on track.

Right now, I'm fortunate in that my avocation is also my vocation; I make a living doing what I love to do. But in a few years, who knows where I'll be? I could be running for office, running a corporation or serving as a missionary. I just don't know. My options, and yours, too, are always open, but I know one thing is certain: If each day I strive for Clarity, my life will be richer for it.

Making Clarity Personal

To jump-start the Clarity process, here are three questions to consider:

1. We talked about three elements of Clarity:

Mission: Why do I exist?
Vision: What do I want to become?
Values: How will I make my choices?

In which of these areas do I need to do the most work right now?

2. What action will I take today to do that work?

3. How will I (and those around me) gain when I grow in Clarity?

Take a minute to reflect on these questions. When you've come up with some good ideas, take action!

Pillar Principle Nine: Integrity

When I was at Cornell University, I had a professor whose name you'll probably recognize: astronomer Carl Sagan. It was the spring of 1978, and he was already famous.

I sat in Uris Hall with 500 other 20-year-olds, waiting to take the final exam in a course I had not liked much. Astronomy 101 was a required course if I wanted to graduate—and I did—but since it was not a subject that interested me, the only good thing about it was having Sagan for a teacher. I squeaked by with the only sub-C grade of my college career.

The day of the exam, Dr. Sagan caught us all off guard. He entered the room, paused for effect and announced that the final had been postponed for three days. How do you think 500 stressed-out college students reacted to that?

There was some serious celebrating going on when a young man I didn't know stood up two seats to my right and asserted loudly, "Professor Sagan, I don't like this at all! I've worked hard to prepare for this test. I know my material. I have five other finals to take, and I'm also working two part-time jobs. I need to take this exam *today!*" He quickly added the words "thank you" and "Sir" to the end of his little speech and sat down, shaking.

The class fell silent. Nobody moved. Wow, most of us were thinking. He just confronted the great Carl Sagan in front of everybody. There goes his grade for the semester. What a dumb thing to do.

Finally, Dr. Sagan spoke. "What is your name, young man?" For a moment, the student just sat there, staring back at the professor. "Ron," he finally answered. "Ron Adams."

"Mr. Adams!" Sagan said, "I am proud of you. Proud of your courage and your willingness to stand up for what you feel is right." The cloud was lifting from the room. "This is what I'll do for you. I won't make you take the final exam, and regardless of your grade up 'til now, I'll give you an A+ for the course."

The stunned crowd began to whisper and murmur. Suddenly, the young man was on his feet again. "Well, thank you very much, Sir," he said. "And if that's the case, my name is really *John Wilson!*"

That story may not be *completely* true, but I love it because of the surprise ending. We're set up for a tale of Courage but it's really about a lack of Integrity. It's a story about a person loudly and proudly proclaiming his beliefs—under someone else's identity. Can you imagine that? Sadly, I'll bet we all can. Maybe we've seen it, and maybe we've done it. Either way, Integrity is our ninth Pillar Principle and we can't live a life of Excellence without it.

We just finished talking about the importance of having Clarity in our lives, and we said that Clarity is, in part, defining what principles we stand for. But once we know what we stand for, we still have to stand. That is the essence of Integrity.

Acting in Accordance with My Beliefs

A colleague, Tom Regnier, told me about a time he jeopardized a long-term consulting relationship with one of his clients. The client serves hundreds of other companies and Tom helps them as needed with specific customers. One day, the president called Tom into his office to give him the good news that he would be working with one of their very good customers, a tobacco company.

Tom froze, but only for a moment. Because he felt strongly about tobacco issues, he quickly summoned the Courage to tell the president he wouldn't work with a tobacco company. After a pause that seemed interminable to Tom, the president finally said with a smile, "Well, I guess we'll just have to find some other work for you to do."

Tom followed up the meeting with an e-mail message thanking the president for his sensitive response. The president answered, saying, "Well, that's the good news about having 200 clients, Tom. There are lots of people you can help us help!"

Tom was clear on the principles that would shape his decisions. But all the Clarity in the world wouldn't have made a bit of difference if he had not taken action on the principles he said he believed in. That's why I use this definition of Integrity:

Acting in accordance with the principles I say I value

Integrity, like the QBQ, involves taking action—action that's in line with the beliefs I claim to hold. Taking action in line with my beliefs is one of the hardest things to do but also one of the most powerful—and it's a key to practicing Personal Accountability.

We're All Role Models

One of the principles *I* value is openness, so I will be open with you right now—embarrassingly so. One day I let my girls have some fun with Dad: I let them dress me up. Don't ask how it got started; I honestly don't recall. But thanks to a full-length mirror in Kristin's bedroom, I'll never forget the image they created: A man in his 30s wearing a short skirt, white blouse, earrings and necklace, lots of makeup, and tight, hot-pink mesh tights over hairy legs. Sorry.

Brother Michael was invited in to see his sisters' masterpiece, and at the age of eight, he took one look at Dad and said, "And this is my male role model?"

It's true: Sons watch dads, daughters watch moms, employees watch managers, scouts watch the troop leader and athletes watch the coach. No matter what our position or situation in life, someone is looking to us for guidance, whether we like it or not. We need to take responsibility for that fact and make sure we're sending messages of Integrity to those around us. It helps to remember this truth (no pun intended, in light of the dress-up session with my daughters):

Modeling is the most powerful of all teachers.

The Message of Integrity

Integrity does not necessarily involve confronting big, controversial issues. Most of the time Integrity is demonstrated in simple little things that in and of themselves may not seem like much, but in fact, send a strong message to others.

Mike Conley was president of a division of ReliaStar Financial when he shared with me a great example of this: "John, I can't talk about cutting costs, tightening our belt and watching our expenses one day, then turn around the next and pay extra for a first-class flight."

Now, I know first-class flights often are given as free upgrades for frequent flyers. But that's not the issue. It was clear to me that Mike understood the message it sent to spend lavishly while asking others to be frugal. He's a great role model for all of us for the Pillar of Integrity.

Closing the Gaps

One way to illustrate symptoms of a lack of Integrity is to talk about the gaps that result when an action does not line up with a stated principle. Gaps can occur in any role we play. Here are some examples I'll bet we've all seen in the various arenas of life. See if any seem familiar.

The salesperson. A sales professional may say, "I exist to help the customer solve problems. I am a consultative salesperson." Back at the office, though, it's a different story. There's talk about "making the pitch," "getting the deal" and earning big commissions. Do you recognize the gap? The self-focused discussion at the office is a far cry from the noble intentions expressed earlier.

I was taught that my language represents my innermost thinking. In other words, the language I use reflects my real thoughts, my true beliefs. Salespeople making pitches and closing deals are not truly interested in building long term relationships with clients and solving the customer's problems. They are in the selling business for all the wrong reasons.

Are we really there to help a client or are we trying to get an order? I've found that when we sincerely focus on the former, the latter works out just fine. One man I met who had been in sales nearly 40 years said to me, "I've never been very good at selling, but *I sure can help people!*"

In the early '70s, Jean sold encyclopedias door to door to earn money for college. She enjoyed the work and wanted to help people learn with the tools she offered. One prospect she visited was a couple about to have their second child. They welcomed her into their tiny house. She observed that it was clean and tidy and that slipcovers on the furniture poorly hid years of wear. The television rested on orange crates and the curtains were made of old sheets.

The young couple was very polite and interested in the product. They asked the kinds of questions that indicated real buying interest. Jean, a gifted salesperson, gave them the whole presentation. The couple signed up for the deluxe package, complete with atlas, annual yearbooks and a two-tiered bookshelf to house their investment.

Jean was happy as she left the house with the down-payment check and a contract for the balance to be paid over the next 12 months. What a great feeling. This sale, on the last day of the month, was bound to impress her boss and colleagues, since it would put her "over the top." She was Number One, Numero Uno, in the district for the first time!

She slipped into her car and pulled out the written agreement, completing the rest of the blanks. The sale's not complete until the paperwork is done, she thought to herself as she flipped through the agreement and checked over the lines and boxes, making sure nothing had been left blank. She saw the "Children" box filled in with a one. "Soon to be two," she said out loud. Then she stopped and looked up from the page.

Jean thought about that young family and their real needs. She unclipped the check and stared at it. "Number One in the district for the first time!" But she knew what she had to do. She smiled and breathed a deep sigh as she ripped up the check, folded the paperwork inside a big white envelope and wrote a message on the back. She put the packet in the couple's mailbox and drove away. The note said, "Thanks for your time and your interest in my product. If I'm still selling encyclopedias in a couple of years, I'll be back to help you out then."

Jean had always said she cared about her customers. Now she had proved it by her actions. No gap there. That's Integrity. Today, as a physician, she continues to care for and about people. Jean is a unique individual.

The manager or executive. How about the middle manager who comes back from the training session on coaching and tells the associates, "I'm your coach and I've discovered my reason for existence: to lift you up, serve you and help you reach your personal goals. Yes, that's why I exist!" But the next day, with doors open and people watching, that same manager is yelling, "When are you going to do the job right?" and "If you don't start hitting your numbers, there'll be Hell to pay!"

What happened to the caring coach?

Or the executive who stands at the lectern before the large corporate audience, stating, "You are empowered, each and every one of you. Show that you're a leader by taking initiative in your work today." Almost in the next breath, however, these words are heard: "Before you do anything in the field, be sure to check with us at headquarters first!" This happens every day somewhere in corporate America, doesn't it?

The employee. I enjoy sharing this message because I sense we are all starving for more Integrity. When we observe Integrity in action, we recognize it and respect it. The problem, though, is that it's so tempting to say, "Yes, Integrity sure is important! When are *all the people around me* going to start walking their talk?"

Many a management team has gone off to the mountaintop retreat to define the corporate mission, vision and values. The team returns with the new philosophy on a little plastic card we can sit on (at least the men can). Then, throughout the organization, cynics say, "Well, I'll live those values when *management* starts living those values. They have to do it first."

No, it begins with me.

The organization. Then there's the company that espouses this message: "People Are Our Greatest Asset." Have you heard that one? We proclaim it as though we really mean it. Yet I learned from Jim Strutton, the man who hired me to sell training, that the average firm spends more dollars landscaping its grounds than developing its people. (Believe me, it's true.)

Many times I've called on vice presidents who escort me to the lobby door after a brief face-to-face visit, saying, "Sorry, John, there's just no money in the budget or time in our hectic schedules for training."

Then, I leave the building, I see a plaque on the wall in the lobby that reads, "People Are Our Greatest Asset."

No, *bushes* are. And trees and grass and fancy sculptures. Let's be honest with ourselves and those around us.

What's down in the well, comes up in the bucket.

The parent. Then there's the parent who says, "I exist to build my children's inner strengths, beliefs and values so they can withstand the challenges of life." But sometimes, out of the fatigue and frustration of everyday living, they turn to their six-year-old, their 16-year-old or their 26-year-old and ask IQs such as these: "Why don't you ever listen to me?" "When are you going to stop being so selfish?" and "Why aren't you more like your sister?"

If I say I'm a great parent, I should be one.

The elected official. What we really need are more "statespeople" in office and fewer politicians. A politician is concerned with the next election, but a statesperson is concerned with the next generation. So often, the politician says, "I exist to help people, to stand on my values and to do what's right. I will ignore the court of public opinion."

Are you sure, Mr. Congressman, Ms. Senator or Mr. President? Let's not be the person licking our index finger every morning, sticking it high in the air and turning to the paid pollster to inquire, "Which way are the winds of opinion blowing today?"

The spouse. The wife says, "I love him just the way he is." But her actions say, "Every chance I get, I'll try to change this guy." Or, perhaps the husband says, "I love you, Karen, just the way you are and appreciate all that you do." But then, he looks at her and says, "Why in the world didn't you ship the Karmelkorn overnight?" I'm glad I didn't ask that question, because it might have led to a "discussion"!

Karen and I were having one such discussion on a Tuesday around 7 p.m. in our bedroom with the door closed. Suddenly, out of frustration, she opened the door to head downstairs. Guess who was there? All four children: Kristin, Tara, Michael and Molly. Ever seen four kids stacked in a column along a doorjamb, oldest to youngest, with hands cupped to their ears? Molly, at that time about six years old, looked at Mom's face, sensed her anger with Dad, and coyly said, "Mom, you gonna ground him?"

Let me say, she didn't ground me.

Being grounded, to use the word in another sense, though, means standing firmly and squarely on what I say I believe in—acting in accordance with the principles I say I value. Can Karen, or anyone else, ground me? No. Can I ground her? No. Can anyone ground someone other than herself? Not a chance! It's my job to close the gaps in all the roles I play.

I don't think most people act out of synch with their convictions intentionally. When we say things such as, "you're empowered" and "I accept you just the way you are," we most likely mean it at the time. But somehow our actions too often end up saying something else entirely. We're blind to the gaps in our own lives. The QBQ that enables me to live a life of Integrity is simply, "What can I do today, in all the roles I play, to bring my actions and my words together?"

QBQ Integrity

What can we do to remedy our Integrity gaps? For starters, let's talk about some of the factors that contribute to these gaps. Perhaps the biggest one is inordinate concern with others' opinions. Or, phrased as an IQ, "Who will approve (or disapprove) of me?"

What I'm really saying when I ask that question is, "If I take this action or say those words, what will those around me think?" This is very natural, of course, since it's good to be civil and strive to please others to a certain extent. But, taken too far, this desire can be a huge hindrance to practicing Personal Accountability. I liken it to having my ankles shackled with a 200-pound iron ball at the end of a heavy 10-foot chain. On the ball is engraved, "The Opinions of Others." Do you drag that ball and chain around with you? I think most of us do, though I have known people to shake it off from time to time.

Going to the Mat

It was the winter of 1974 and my dad was about to close his final year as Cornell's wrestling coach. The last meet of the season was against Princeton, and the winner would take home the best record in the Ivy League and the championship. It usually was Cornell or Princeton, making for an exciting rivalry.

Every bout in that meet was close. As the night progressed, our fear was that the meet would come down to the heavyweight bout, since Princeton's heavyweight was the best in the conference and Cornell's was, well, "challenged" at this weight class. His name was Mark and he really had chosen the wrong sport. The best heavyweights combine size, strength and quickness, and they're hard to find. Unfortunately, Mark's only attribute was his weight.

Going into the final bout, our fears were realized. Cornell was ahead, but only by five points. In collegiate wrestling, you pin your opponent if you hold both his shoulder blades to the mat for one full second. For that, your team gets six points. The only way Princeton could win the meet and take home the Ivy League championship—not to mention the bragging rights—was if their man pinned Mark.

It goes without saying that few in Barton Hall that night wanted to see that happen. It was a partisan home-town crowd. The coach's family, the Millers, was rooting and pacing with every move on the mat. If Mark could avoid getting pinned, we'd win the championship by one point. Given the rules of amateur wrestling at that time, he could lose by lots of points—as long as he didn't get pinned—and our team would still win. Could he do it? We all knew the odds were against us.

From the start of his match, there were no surprises. True to form, Mark was on his back from the first minute with the referee right there, watching and counting, ready to slap the mat and blow the whistle. This was going to be the longest bout we had ever watched, but that, of course, was better than the shortest bout we had ever watched!

The crowd was screaming, almost in unison, "Mark, stay off your back!" The roar was deafening. From my experience as a wrestler, I knew Mark couldn't hear us—but there was no doubt he knew what he had to do.

The clock was winding down on the nine-minute match. Fifteen seconds. If the referee didn't slap the mat, Cornell would win. Ten seconds. Mark had been struggling and the crowd had been agonizing for what seemed like a lifetime. The fans were all still screaming at the top of their lungs. Five, four, three, two, one. The horn blew. We'd won!

There was one problem, though: Nobody could hear the horn, including the man in the black-and-white-striped shirt. He was still down on his stomach, where he'd spent most of the match, measuring the millimeters between Mark's back and the mat.

The fans were still screaming things at the ref such as, "Why can't you hear the buzzer?" and "When are you going to blow the whistle?" Meanwhile, someone else—my mom, the coach's wife—made a different choice in the moment.

Suddenly, thousands of fans saw Mary Miller, all 110 pounds of her, on the mat with a one-arm choke-hold on the referee, trying to pull two sweaty, confused, 225-pounders apart. What a picture! The next day the *Ithaca Journal*, the local newspaper, ran a photo with a caption that read, "Big Red Coach's Wife Saves the Day!"

This may be a fun story and a great image. But, lest we miss the point, we need to consider why her action demonstrated a better choice in the moment. She wasn't concerned with the opinions of others. She was only concerned with what she believed in. And she didn't hesitate to act, and act boldly. She never asked, "Who will approve (or disapprove) of me?" She went to the mat for her conviction.

Act Boldly

I did a session on the QBQ for a school district and during a break, a middle school principal shared a situation. "I really believe in your 360-Degree Customer Concept," she said, "and I have at least two groups of customers. One is my staff, the teachers and paraprofessionals. The other is the parents and, of course, their children. I have a boy in the sixth grade whose parents want me to move him to another class because they don't care for his teacher, but my staff advises me not to start moving kids around on a parental whim or it'll open a can of worms and we'll have a real mess. What should I do?"

Well, what should she do? The simple answer: She should do what *she* believes is right. I told her we'd soon be covering some content on the Pillar Principle of Integrity that might help her and she returned to her seat. An hour later, when we finished, she approached with a smile and winked at me, saying she'd made her decision. I have no idea what it was, but I do know this: It was *her* decision, and that's what Integrity is all about. Integrity means standing on what we say we believe, taking those tough positions, holding firm against the strong winds of opinion.

The Answer's Not *Blowing in the Wind*

Another version of the struggle with "The Opinions of Others," is peer pressure. In the chapter on Ownership, we heard, "A poor sailor blames the wind." This is also true: *A weak sailor blows in the wind.*

Buffeted by the gusts of prevailing public opinion, the excuse maker and the poor performer decline to choose their own course. That's a picture of peer pressure, and it's especially tough, of course, for teens.

I had a rare opportunity to speak in Atlanta to about 5,000 teens at a conference sponsored by P.R.I.D.E. (Parents Resource Institute for Drug Education). I was given a half-hour to deliver a QBQ message that would be helpful, meaningful and, I hoped, enduring. My first instinct was to tell the teens they are simply too concerned with what others think. Maybe I'd say they blow in the wind too easily, and they need to be stronger. But I couldn't do it. I couldn't say those things. Why? Because I suffer from the same problem. As a man once said to me, "When I lose ten pounds, I'll start warning others about the dangers of being overweight!" If I'm going to tell others to ignore the winds, well, I think you know what I must do first.

Integrity Begins with Me

I believe in the saying, "We tend to teach to others what *we* need to hear the most." We've spent a lot of time talking about the importance of acting with Integrity, and I want you to know that *I* know this message is as much for me as for anyone. There's no better way to communicate this than to tell you about a time I really blew it.

On a Saturday in December, my wife and our four kids piled into our van and headed for a local mall to do some holiday shopping. Traffic was heavy. The crew was getting hungry, so we decided to stop at the McDonald's next to the mall. We negotiated our way into the left-turn lane and got stuck at a red light.

A man was standing on the corner at the intersection. He was proba bly in his mid-40s, had a full beard and stood about six feet tall. He was wearing a well-worn army jacket, ripped jeans, tennis shoes, a skimpy wool hat and gloves with holes in their fingers. This was hard-ly sufficient covering for December in Minnesota.

I probably wouldn't have noticed all these details had it not been for the cardboard sign he was holding that said, "Food for work." Our kids had never seen such a sign and they had a lot of questions. Karen and I did our best to answer them. "Yes, kids, he's probably hungry. Yeah, I guess he'd work for food, not just money. No, he probably has no place to go tonight. Yes, I'm sure he's poor. No, he probably does not have a home. I'm sure he's cold. You're right, it's very sad."

Finally, the light changed and we turned into the home of 660 Billion Served, or whatever the sign said that year.

Now, if you've spent any time with children in restaurants, you know that ordering fast food is not an exact science. By the time the fourth child had ordered, the first child had changed her mind about nine times. Talk about confusing. (Sometimes I wonder if this is where traders on the stock exchange floor get their training!)

Finally, we placed an order, and after 30 minutes of heavy eating and light conversation, we walked out. I was carrying a leftover cheeseburger, still warm in the wrapper, untouched. We got into the van, turned around and pulled up to the same red light. The "Food for work" guy was still there. He hadn't moved.

Suddenly, Kristin—the missionary in our family—who was nine years old at the time, asked the question I did not want to hear. From the back bench of our van she shouted out, "Daddy, can you get out and give that guy our left-over cheeseburger? We don't need it."

I froze. And my 200-pound ball and chain suddenly swelled to 2,000 pounds. I made my choices in that moment and did some fast talking. I said things such as, "Well, Kristin, it's awfully cold. The light's about to turn green. Might cause an accident. I've got lots of cars behind me. I'm sure he wouldn't accept charity, anyway!" An eternity passed and the light turned green. As we pulled away, the man and I exchanged a glance, and then we were gone.

Many years later, I vaguely remember his face, but there is another face I cannot forget. About a quarter mile down the road, as the man with the sign disappeared into our past, I looked in the rear view mirror and what do you think I saw? The face of a nine-year-old with freckles, dazzling green eyes and a tear coming down each cheek because she'd just seen her daddy refuse to feed a hungry man. There was no refuting, denying or wishing it away. She saw what she saw.

For a moment, let's put aside our politics, our opinions on social programs and our temptation to wonder whether the man would have taken the food. People have said to me, "Well, maybe he was a con man," which honestly had never occurred to me. Even if that were true, it's beside the point. What this moment in time represented to me was a daughter watching her daddy *not* stand on his stated values. *Not* live what he said he claimed to believe. *Not* follow his own teachings. *Not* demonstrate Integrity.

You see, at home, standing in the nice, warm kitchen of our comfortable house with food at our fingertips from Oreos to fresh fruit, from peanut butter to pork chops, I had been throwing around words such as "sharing," "giving," "tithing" and "helping those less fortunate." These were messages I thought bore constant repeating. Nevertheless, my actions in that moment were completely inconsistent with those words; I didn't share, give or help.

Quite candidly, as easy as it is to use words like sharing, giving and helping, it was just as easy *not* to feed the hungry man. Yes, you read that right. I'm not saying I *almost* fed the hungry man. Or, I was within an inch of feeding the hungry man. I don't claim that I *wanted* to feed the hungry man. In fact, I don't believe, in that moment, I even considered doing so. Even under the pressure of Kristin's pointed question, "Daddy, can you get out and give that guy our left-over cheeseburger?" I wasn't tempted to do what was right.

Why? Because I was asking the wrong question: "Who will approve (or disapprove) of me? There are people everywhere. If I stop traffic, get out, run 20 feet and hand this man our cheeseburger, I'll look like a total fool." That's what was really on my mind, and it demonstrates the amazing power we give the opinions of others.

At 15, I asked Kristin the essence of her memory from that day. "I remember looking out the back window, Dad, as we drove away," she said, "and I just felt really bad deep down inside for that cold, lonely man. He looked so sad." Ouch. Well, I asked.

As unpleasant as that memory is for me, it also helps me by reminding me of the big difference between my words and my actions. I realize I need to be vigilant constantly if I want to live a life I'm proud of and be a good role model for those around me. It helps me in my mission, too. I simply could not stand up and talk about Courage and Integrity and the power of Personal Accountability if I didn't do my best every day to practice those same principles in my own life. Do I come up short sometimes? Of course I do. But, like you, I am committed to living in accordance with the principles I say I value even when it is not easy.

Seeing Sermons

Acting with Integrity begins with me, because each of us can only teach by example. I'd like to share with you a poem my dad once gave me that sums it all up beautifully.

Sermons We See

I'd rather see a sermon than to hear one any day.
I'd rather one should walk with me than just to show the way.
The eye is a better pupil and more willing than the ear;
Advice may be misleading but examples are always clear.
And the very best of teachers are the ones who live their creeds,
For to see good put into action is what everybody needs.
I can soon learn to do it if you'll let me see it done.
I can watch your hand in motion, but your tongue too fast may run.
And the lectures you deliver may be very fine and true,
But I'd rather get my lesson by observing what you do.
For I may misunderstand you and the fine advice you give,
But there's no misunderstanding how you act and how you live!

Edgar A. Guest

Does that touch you? It does me, perhaps because as a father, husband, friend, salesperson, son, brother, speaker and author, I sometimes fall into the trap of giving—rather than living—sermons. I know I can do better. How about you?

Making Integrity Personal

I'll leave us with three QBQs to help us be better role models, act on our stated beliefs and live out the Pillar of Integrity.

1. What must I do differently to live my life by the principles I say I value?

2. In which specific role(s) I play, do I need to close the gap between my actions and my words?

3. What specific action can I take today that reflects my stated values and beliefs?

And one final thought:

People possessing personal power persistently practice professed principles.

Pillar Principle Ten: Belief

In 1967 my father received quite an honor. The United States Olympic Committee asked him to coach the USA wrestling team in the Pan American Games. This competition involving North, Central and South American countries is considered an important pre-Olympic test.

One of the wrestlers was a young man from Oregon named Richie Sanders. Richie had a dry sense of humor and a quick wit. He was the proverbial class clown. And when it came to competing on the mat, he was one of the best. In these games he made it all the way to the finals. Unfortunately, his opponent in the gold-medal bout was one of Cuba's best wrestlers ever. If you know anything about amateur wrestling, you know that's saying a lot.

Richie was losing to the Cuban 11-2 when, in the last minute, he caught an elbow in the nose. The referee stepped in, broke the match and sent Richie over to his corner where the trainer worked to clean him up.

My dad, the Great Motivator, gave Richie some patented "Jimmy Miller" coaching: "Richie, you're doin' great out there! I'm so proud of you! You're an inspiration to everybody on this team!"

Richie, not feeling inspirational, just looked at my Dad and tried to catch his breath. Dad continued, "I'm so glad you're part of this team. You're a great role model for the rest of the guys." Richie glanced up and through the blood, sweat and tears read the scoreboard: Cuba 11, USA 2, with 58 seconds to go. He shook his head.

Dad wasn't fazed. "Richie, you're terrific! I know you can beat this guy. In fact, he hasn't even laid a hand on you!"

Richie didn't say anything for a moment as the trainer finished cleaning him up. Then the team clown smiled a small smile and said, "Well, Coach, if that's the case, when I go back out there on the mat, keep your eyes on the *referee*, 'cause somebody's killing me out there!"

The great part of that story is that Richie did go back out on the mat, and with less than a minute left, he pinned the Cuban wrestler, winning the match and the gold medal. In fact, all eight wrestlers that year brought home gold for the USA. It was a proud moment for our country and for everyone involved—the eight young men, their families, my Dad and lots of fans.

Years later, I asked my Dad what he thought made that team so special and he summed it up in one word: Belief. They believed in themselves, they believed in their team, they were proud to be representing their country and they knew what winning would mean to everyone.

Our tenth and final Pillar Principle, Belief, is the great multiplier, the secret weapon that gives us the extra boost we need to keep moving toward our vision. Given two competitors with equal talents and abilities, whether individuals, teams or organizations, the one with the most Belief has the advantage. If we want to thrive in today's world, we need to develop and strengthen our Belief.

Defeating the Thief

Belief is like theft insurance. There are many "thieves" at work in the world: unreturned phone calls, broken promises, sales that fall through, relational struggles, fear, frustrations, hurts, unkind words, health problems, market competition and the winds of change, to name a few. I call them thieves because they steal my greatest gift: my energy. Think about it. Without my enthusiasm, passion and energy, how can I make a difference each day? In fact, how can I make it *through* the day? I cannot.

When thieves steal my energy, I lose the will to make the next sales call, confront a tough issue with the team, improve the relationship that needs more Trust or face a new problem. I'm sure that Richie, with a bloody nose and an 11-to-2 deficit, wasn't looking forward to going back out on that mat. But by practicing the Pillar Principle of Belief, he was able to dig down deep and find the strength to defeat the thieves. Write this down and remember it:

My only relief from the thief is my Belief.

Let's explore how we can develop and strengthen our Belief, because that's what people who practice Personal Accountability do every day.

QBQ Belief

The question we never want to ask is the IQ, "Who outside of me will define, shape and build my beliefs?" Now that's probably not the question we'd ask in exactly those words, but we do ask it: "When is someone going to train me?" "Who's going to support me more?" "Why doesn't all this change go away?" Sometimes, I unwittingly expect others to infuse Belief into me. In reality, that's *my* job!

Belief is something we can only build for ourselves. The QBQ is this: "What can I do today to strengthen my beliefs?" To practice Personal Accountability through the Pillar of Belief, we need to work in four areas, the same four in which Dad's Pan American Games champions demonstrated Belief: myself, my teammates, my organization and my value—the contribution I make to others' lives.

1. Myself

The young son about to run his first race said to his mother, "You mean, Mom, if I really believe in myself I can win this race?" She responded wisely, "Son, if you believe in yourself, you've already won!" First, I must possess Belief in myself.

We all choose where to work. We may not always feel as if we do, but no one comes to our house every morning, ties us up and drags us to work. We choose to go. We can probably state the reasons we go: "Here's why I choose to work at Organization XYZ." But can we answer the question in reverse? "What causes Organization XYZ to choose *me?*" Or, for the self-employed, "What causes my customers to choose to work with me?" Can we list those talents and abilities? The answers to these questions are a vehicle to strengthen our personal confidence and Belief.

I'd like to recommend an exercise. Write down on paper your five main talents, skills, gifts and strengths. Be specific. Don't just write, "I'm a nice person!" Too general. Instead, write out, "I have the gift of compassion and can listen patiently to others when they need a friend," or "I have the ability to see the big picture and communicate it to others" or "I am very good at encouraging my teammates." Go ahead and have fun with this exercise. Remember, be specific.

Most people have a hard time with this exercise, primarily because so many of us have been taught that certainty equates to cockiness, surety to self-importance and confidence to conceit. We're told, "Now, don't be too sure of yourself!" and we take it to heart. I've taken many a group through this exercise and I'm amazed at how often people cannot, in specific language, articulate their own strengths.

Another reason is that we're not *asked* very often what we're good at. Performance reviews, training programs and we ourselves tend to focus more on our weaknesses. If it helps, ask someone you trust to appraise your abilities (notice the word "praise"?). Just getting a fresh perspective can make a difference. Often, others see our talents more clearly and more quickly than we do.

I hope we'll be able to get a better sense of our own strengths through this little exercise. Knowing and celebrating our strengths is an important part of building Belief in self.

Viewing Others, Viewing Self

Another big part of believing in ourselves is how we view ourselves in relation to others. I often see three levels of Belief, demonstrated in attitudes that are "too hot," "too cold" and "just right."

The "too hot" attitude is exemplified in superiority. The salesperson sends the prospect the message, "I'm the expert here and without me you'll never survive!" The manager signals the employee, "I'm the Omnipotent Big Kahuna around here! Can't you tell? The sign on my desk says "Supervisor" and I have all the answers!" The parent says, "As long as you're in this house and I'm paying the bills, you'll live by my rules and do exactly as I say!" The friend says, "If you keep trying real hard you can be more like me!" We chuckle over these, but they happen. I'll bet you've encountered some of them yourself.

The "too cold" attitude is represented by inferiority. It is evident when I somehow communicate to the customer, "Oh, please, my Great and Mighty One, grant me a sale today so I can be validated as worthy in your sight and in the sight of others in my life from whom I draw my entire significance!"

Another example is a manager who doesn't dare confront a highly productive team member about a behavior that is having an adverse impact on the team. The manager thinks, "If I talk to her she might quit, and where would I be without my top person? I might fail!" Sad, but it happens too often. We coddle one individual to the detriment of the entire organization.

In contrast, the "just right" attitude is operating when we view those around us as peers. A peer is defined as "one of equal standing."

A few years ago, I learned something about peers from Dr. Michael O'Connor. He is a psychologist and a co-author with Ken Blanchard. He also conducts values-based training for corporations. At the time of our meeting, I was 37. Michael told me that as most people approach 40 they stop looking for mentors and begin searching out colleagues. Intriguing, I thought. "What's the difference?" I asked him.

"A mentor is someone I learn *from*. A colleague is someone I learn *with*," he said.

People who feel inferior obviously don't see others as colleagues, because they have a hard time believing they have something to teach. Conversely, have you noticed that people who act superior frequently are covering for a feeling of inferiority? People who have a healthy level of Belief in themselves tend to view others as colleagues, equals and peers. They seek to learn together.

Just imagine the difference it would make if instead of toiling under the typical, top-down Dilbert model, my manager and I looked at each other as peers who are there to swap knowledge and wisdom so we can grow as a team together. Think what we could accomplish if we asked the QBQ, "How can I treat those around me as equals?"

To strengthen my Belief in myself, I need to spend some time thinking about my own strengths and abilities, and developing that "just right" attitude of viewing those around me as peers. Let's face it, if *I* don't have Belief in myself, who will?

2. My Teammates

Second, I must believe in my teammates. My team, in this sense, could be those who fit the 360-Degree Customer Concept from the Pillar of Service chapter—anyone! We need to believe in each other, and we also need to express and demonstrate that Belief to each other. It's amazing what a solid message of Belief can do.

A good friend, Miles Canning, who is a writer and trainer, told me about an exercise he saw in a high school leadership workshop that illustrates this point. First, the facilitators gathered the kids randomly into twelve groups of five. Then each group was told it had forty seconds to elect one person in the group to do a standing broad jump. All the jumpers would compete from the same line on the gym floor. Elections were held, jumps were made and measurements were taken.

Each team was then given 60 seconds to convince the jumper he or she could jump farther next time. Pandemonium erupted as sixty kids started shouting their encouragements: "You can do it, you're the best, relax, think distance, float like a butterfly, we're behind you, come on, go, go, go!" After a minute of that, the jumpers tried to beat their first jump, and amazingly, *every* one of them exceeded the first mark, some by more than a foot. Do you believe the team's message of Belief was instrumental to the results? I do.

Who in your life could benefit from making a longer jump? Let's root them on today. As a result, I'll bet they will exceed their old marks, too. I know I have.

Start Seeing 20

In February 1986, Jim Strutton hired me to sell training for The Fortune Group. My first assignment was to sell 20 sales managers on attending a $500, two-day workshop to be held in May. I learned to sell fast. I was cold-calling by phone, digging up leads, working hard. By May, though, only nine people had signed up. On the day of the workshop, I was discouraged. Jim would facilitate the session while I watched and learned, so we set up the room together—nine chairs around a "U" of tables—and then had a few minutes to wait for the customers to arrive.

Jim looked over the room and said, "You know what, John, I see 20." Slightly confused I said, "Twenty what, Jim?"

"I see 20 managers in this class," he answered.

"Jim," I said, trying to straighten him out, "I only sold nine tickets!"

Then this wise man looked me in the eye and said, "I know that, John, but I see twenty because I know *you* can do it!"

We held the class and I learned a great deal. The material was also a Belief-builder for me as I saw some sales managers' lives changed. One told me he'd been ready to throw in the towel as a manager and go back into the field, but our workshop renewed his hope and confidence. It had the same effect on me.

We had another session scheduled for July, 60 days later, and I never worked so hard in my life. I had to call on my Courage and expand my comfort zone daily. I also got lots of practice learning not to internalize rejection. Good thing too, because otherwise the thief would've made it all too easy to quit. If you've ever been in sales, I'll bet you know exactly what I mean.

I remember one day in particular when after making 75 phone calls, reaching only a half-dozen prospects and being turned down by all of them, I sat alone in my office (a furnace room in the basement of my house), lay my head on my desk, and muttered, "Wow, this is impossible."

July arrived. I had sold 16 tickets. Better, but still short of the objective of twenty. Again, Jim came up to me before the session began and said, "John, I see 20."

"No, Jim," I said this time, "Do your math. There are only 16 chairs in this room!" Again, just as before, he said, "I know that, but I see 20, because I know *you* can do it." OK, Jim, maybe I can. Maybe I can.

One month later, in August of 1986, I conducted a class for twenty-two managers, and for the next two years never had a class with fewer than twenty. Yes, I needed to possess Belief in myself and my potential, but I also needed someone in my life to help me develop that Belief. I needed someone to transfer his Belief *in* me *to* me. This is a rare skill and it's called encouraging the heart.

Jim helped propel me to Excellence by sending a powerful and genuine message, "I Believe in you!" I heard that message loud and clear. It made all the difference in the world—and it encouraged my heart, too.

What messages are you sending to the people around you? Too often, I think, instead of "I see 20," we send a message of doubt. Here are some examples:

- "Did you check your numbers?"

- "You've got to be kidding, you want to be a musician? Your mother and I want you to be a physician!"

- "You handled that customer call how?"

- "Why do you want to go to that college? That's not where I would go if I were you!"

- "Why did you do the project that way?"

- "Come back to me with three options and we'll make the decision together."

Do you hear the messages of doubt? Each in its own way says, "I doubt your capabilities." I don't think we mean it that way, necessarily, but as with the Pillar of Integrity, we don't always realize the underlying messages our words and actions send. One good way I've found to keep the "I see 20" perspective is to ask the QBQ, "How can I help others help themselves today?"

I always felt like Jim's teammate, his colleague. As my mentor, he taught me a lot, but gradually we started learning *together*. The Belief he transferred to me is a gift I carry yet today. Who in your life needs that gift from you right now? Write down their name(s), go to them and tell them in one way or another, "I see 20, because I know *you* can do it!"

As they walk away, take a look at their feet and you'll notice their shoes will not even be touching the floor. It's possible that for the first time in their lives, they heard total acceptance, support and Belief. No coded words that say, "I'll believe in you when you change!" Just Belief in who and what they are today. Now that's encouraging the heart!

Start developing Belief in your team by practicing the "I see 20" outlook toward others and demonstrating that Belief with your words and your actions. And remember, when someone on your team does well, you do well, too.

3. My Organization

Beyond Belief in self and teammates, those who practice Personal Accountability have Belief in the organization they represent. My dad's wrestlers were proud to represent the United States and their pride was an important part of the strength that helped them succeed. We too need that kind of Belief, represented by our actions and our words, in our organization.

Jay Leno tells a story about when he was a young stand-up comedi-an. After his show he would stand at the exit door and as they left, people would say, "Great show, Jay, great show. Very funny, terrific show, Jay." He would nod, shake their hands and thank everybody. Then he began to wonder, "Are they really telling the truth?" Right after his routines, he began to slip out and make his way to the place truth can be found. Yes, you guessed it—the rest room.

He'd enter a stall in the men's room, close the door, put his feet up on a toilet and listen. He would hear good things of course, because he *is* funny, but he'd also hear some critical things that people would never say to his face. Can you imagine that? People saying one thing to his face and something else out of earshot, so they thought. He began to make it a regular practice to head for the bathroom after his routines so he could get some honest feedback.

Now, if I ever speak at your organization, you'll know where to find me immediately following my program! (That does make me wonder how Jay got women's opinions.)

Why do I bring up Jay's method of getting feedback? One reason is that I've seen the same thing happen in organizations over and over again.

As you know, I've spent a lot of time facilitating and speaking to groups of people in all kinds of organizations. Often, a team will put a vision statement on the wall, point to it and say, "Yes, we can do that and we can be that! We're the biggest, the best and the boldest!"

Then we'll take a break to go out in the hall for a cup of coffee, and someone will come up to me—the neutral outsider—and whisper something that sounds a lot like this: "We'll never do it! We have bad products, poor management, lousy morale and no vision."

To me, this is the ultimate gap: to sit in a meeting and essentially say, "I believe!" then walk outside and mutter, "I don't believe!"

Do you have Belief in your organization? I don't mean blind Belief. I remember one vice president standing up at the lectern for a national sales meeting with a group that was having severe Belief problems. I thought he was going to spend the whole evening bellowing into the microphone, "Do you believe?" while 300 people nodded and yelled back, "Yes, we believe!"

The problem was, they didn't believe. I'd done enough consulting work there to know that for a fact.

Organizations have problems. We all know that. We can disguise them with euphemisms such as "challenges," "issues," "roadblocks" and the big one, "opportunities," but they're still problems that need solving. So I'm not saying, "Rah-rah, everything's great!" as in, "Let's pretend there's nothing wrong."

We need to take an honest look at ourselves and our organizations. Sometimes positive thinking borders on denial. I do believe that what we can conceive and believe, we can achieve, but we also should be very careful about "positive thinking." Positive thinking can create a frustrating and impossible ideal to maintain.

Let's employ *optimistic* thinking, with optimism defined as this:

A complete awareness of problems, wrapped in an attitude of solution

Believe Your Stated Belief

Here's a question only you can answer: Does what you say about your organization while you're at work match what you say at home?

If not, that's a problem. That's a crack in your Belief and represents a thief that is going to steal your energy until you reconcile the beliefs you claim at work with those you share at home.

It may sound a little harsh, but some day I'd like to come into a meeting and see a big banner on the wall that says, "Believe or Leave!" Now, I'm not saying, "Believe or you're a bum!" I'm just saying if we don't believe, maybe it would be better if we moved on. Better for the organization, yes, but better for each of us, too.

And by the way, let's stop shooting people verbally as they walk out the door, shall we? Do you know what I mean? "Oh, he's no longer with us? Good thing, he wasn't cutting it!" And, "She's not part of the team anymore? Well, she didn't really fit in with our culture!" Let's not do that. It's OK to leave.

About a week after I presented the QBQ to a small industrial firm in Ohio, I got an e-mail message from the president. The "Believe or Leave" philosophy had been part of the presentation and his e-mail to me said they'd had four resignations in the days since my talk. "Uh oh," I thought as I read the note, but he went on to say, "John, this is one of the healthiest things that has happened to us in a long time!"

I responded with a question: "Would you rather have had those particular people stay with your organization?"

To my surprise, he shot back a message that said, "I wish three of them had stayed, but it's better they've moved on if this is not the right place for them!" Now that is a mature mind-set on his part. That's the leadership thinking that characterizes Personal Accountability.

And Belief is the key. Organizations need people who believe, and individuals need to work for organizations they believe *in*. When people decide to depart from our organizations, I believe the right thing to do is applaud them. "Congratulations and good for you! You've come to the point where this organization is no longer a vehicle to help you reach your personal vision. That took Clarity—and Courage, too. Thanks for being honest. Best of luck. Stay in touch. As for me, though, I'm staying!"

Please hear me on this: Stay only if you believe. It always amazes me when people stay inside an organization and say negative things. We have all chosen our organizations. If we don't want to be there, we should either change what we can, get over it or leave. Why keep doing something that's not working? It just doesn't make sense—and besides, it hurts business.

My mentor Steve Brown taught me successful selling has less to do with products, programs, polices, procedures, pricing and plans than with the transfusion of Belief. By that I mean that if my prospects have half the Belief I have in what I'm offering, they'll buy. And if they don't, it's either because I didn't communicate my Belief effectively or I never had it in the first place. It's that simple. Successful selling is a transfusion of Belief, from me to you.

If you're thinking, "Well, I'm not in sales," think again. We're all in sales in one way or another. Especially when you think of sales as helping people solve problems. For example, if you now believe in the QBQ *half* as much as I do, you'll use it to practice Personal Accountability. If you believe *three-quarters* as much as I do, you'll start telling everyone you know about it. If your Belief matches mine, it'll enable you to use the QBQ to accomplish positive and permanent change in your life.

Not only are we all in sales, we also serve as ambassadors to the world for our organizations. Since we've chosen to work for our organizations, it's our job to represent them well. When we genuinely believe in what we're doing, being great ambassadors comes naturally.

Want to evaluate your level of Belief in your organization? First, get some Clarity on where you want to be. Is this organization the vehicle to help you reach your personal goals? If so, make sure you're coming to work every day and asking the right questions, the QBQs, "How can I contribute?" "What can I do to make a difference?" and "How can I solve the problem?"

If this is not the organization for you, commit to start looking for a better fit. Whatever you do, don't stay and ask the wrong questions: "When are they going to train me?" "Why don't others do their job?" "Who made the mistake?" "When is all this change going to go away?" Staying and asking the wrong questions is counterproductive because it's a waste of a job, a career—a lifetime! We need to possess and demonstrate our Belief in our organizations.

4. My Value

Lastly, we need to possess Belief in the value we add to the lives of others. Really understanding the difference we make for others is a great source of inspiration to keep us going when the thieves are working to steal our energy. And we can add value to others' lives in countless ways.

Those who add value tend to have careers, as opposed to jobs. They are not clock watchers, but calendar watchers. They're not concerned with the minutes ticking slowly off the clock each day; they just see the years flying by. Do you know what I mean? If not, just go to any office building on a Monday morning and ride the elevator. You'll hear clock watchers say, "Is it really Monday already?" "Where did the weekend go?" "Boy, is this gonna be a long day!" and "I can't believe it's two days till 'hump day.' I'll never make it!" Those people have jobs.

These comments remind me of the bumper sticker, "I owe, I owe, so off to work I go!" Have you seen that? The sad truth is, millions of working people hate their jobs, feel trapped in their careers, or feel under-employed, under-utilized, under-appreciated and miserable about what they do each day, every day, all day.

But the people who focus on the value they bring to others' lives look forward to their work. They have careers, and take great pleasure and pride in making a difference in people's lives, regardless of whether they are doctors, teachers or sanitation workers. Everyone adds value in one way or another.

After speaking for General Motors in Panama City, I encountered a cab driver who was a "52-year-old hippie"—his words, not mine. Not that he needed to tell me. He had a pony tail flowing down his back, love beads around his neck and an old peace symbol pinned to the visor of his cab.

As soon as we started talking, I knew he had a sense of humor. When he learned I lived in Minnesota (at the time), he quickly stated, "Oh, man, I could never live there. We Florida boys freeze at room temperature!"

Beyond the humor, I found some wisdom.

"Sometimes people get into my car and right off the bat apologize to me," he told me. "They say 'I'm really sorry, but I only have to go a mile or two!' So I turn to them in the back seat and say, 'Well, do you gotta go?' Then they look at me kind of funny, so I say again, "Do you have to go that mile or two?' Then they'll say, 'Well, yeah, of course!' And so I say, 'Well, let's do it, *together!*'"

Does he add value? You bet he does. By getting people where they need to go—even when a shorter distance means a smaller fare—and sharing his energy and enthusiasm with every person who climbs into his cab. Which brings to mind another point: People with Belief seem to enjoy life more. He wasn't asking IQs such as, "Why don't I get a better job?" "When will I get a bigger fare?" and "Who does the customer think he is?" His Belief in the value he brings helps him defeat those thieves every day.

Selling with Belief

John McMunn believes in the value he delivers to others. He's a self-employed organizational consultant and he received a phone call one day from the vice president of sales at a large corporation. "John, I was referred to you by one of your clients and we're thinking of using you. Can you tell me what kind of things you do, how you do them and what your fees are?"

John is an excellent salesperson and soon had the prospective customer talking about his company's critical business problems. About an hour later, they agreed John would facilitate some workshops for senior executives. Then the vice president asked—again—the dreaded question: "How much?" John didn't hesitate, "Fifty thousand dollars."

After an awkward pause (probably while picking himself up off the floor), he repeated, "Fifty thousand dollars?"

John replied, "I know it sounds like a lot of money, but your problems are costing you much, much more!"

Now that's selling with Belief. Then John added, "If you feel you can't afford this, let me give you the names of three people in my industry and their phone numbers. I don't know how they will approach your situation, but they're good people and I trust them." The man took down the three names and numbers, thanked John and quickly hung up.

Guess what? One hour later the same vice president called John back. "John, we'd like to do business with you." When John told me this I had to ask, "John, did you ask him whether he called your competitors?"

He replied, "Well, it didn't feel like the right thing to do at that moment, but let me tell you the rest of the story."

A month later, John did the first workshop and he did ask the question. The new client said, "When I got off the phone with you that day, I went down the hall and met with our president. I told him what you had said. His immediate response was, 'What? When you balked at his fee, he didn't sputter and stutter? He didn't stumble and mumble? He didn't offer to cut his price?'

"'No,' I said, 'He gave me these names and numbers of his competitors and said they were worth a call.'

"'Well,' said the president, 'Isn't that the kind of Belief we want our salespeople to have? Isn't that the way we hope our people will respond to a price objection?'

"'Yes,' I said, 'it is!' and he said, 'So go book that man!' I called you back and that was that!"

They hired John not because he was the smartest or the best consultant in the world—though he might be—or because of fate, the winds of fortune or just plain luck. They chose him for one reason: his intense and obvious Belief in the value he brings.

Value that Transforms Lives Forever

On May 20, 1975, when I was just 16, my father showed up unexpectedly at the grocery store gas station where I had a part-time job after school. He was in his pickup truck with my older brother, E.J., and neither of them looked very good. Dad's face was beet red and E.J. was white as a ghost. I'll never forget the contrast. Dad said, "Johnny, I want you to ride home with us." I told him I'd take a raincheck since I had my own car. (Remember the '62 Rambler?)

"No, ride home with us," he insisted sternly.

"But why, Dad?" I asked. I didn't understand. Yet I sensed something was terribly wrong, and I soon discovered my life was about to be altered forever.

"What's going on?" I probed. He had caught me out in the parking lot of the grocery store I worked for right as my shift ended.

"Your mother just died." My dad said the heavy words simply.

I couldn't believe it. I wouldn't believe it. In a futile attempt to deny what I knew I had heard, I said, "Oh, you mean *Grandma* died. Right, Dad?" My mom's mother was in her 80s.

"No," he said, gently, "Mom passed away about an hour ago."

She was 51 years old, and had suffered a sudden cerebral hemorrhage. It's been all these years now but I still miss her, and would give anything for her to know Karen and Kristin, Tara, Michael and Molly.

My seventeenth birthday was May 28, a week after she passed away. All my life, Mom had been the one to create the birthday atmosphere in our house. With all the things going on that week, I didn't know if anyone even realized it was my birthday. I just about forgot, myself. As I drove off the farm for school that morning—my first day back—my father was at the end of the driveway, digging a big hole, I think for a tree. In reality, he was probably trying to stay busy. We spoke, but he didn't mention my birthday and I didn't either, so I just drove on. It was a lonely day.

Around 10:00 a.m., over the intercom at Ithaca High School, I heard, "John Miller, please come to the principal's office." When I got there, I saw on the secretary's desk a long white envelope. On the outside, written in the black flair pen Dad always used, was my name. I knew what it was. You do, too. I opened it up and it said something as simple as, "Dear Johnny, Happy 17th. I love you, Son. We'll get through this!" It was signed "Pop" and inside was a $10 bill he couldn't really afford to give away.

To this day, I can hardly imagine what it must have been like for him to have suddenly lost his best friend of more than 25 years. Yet with all he had on his mind and heart, he set aside his farm work, changed his clothes, drove seven miles to Rexall Drug, bought and filled out the card, drove three more miles to Ithaca High and delivered the surprise—all to show he loved me.

The money is long gone. The memory, and the *value* he added to my life, remain forever. In spite of the incredible thieves he had working against him, he knew what a difference it would make for me, so he dug down deep and found the strength to do it.

We all add value to the lives of others. Not in such a dramatic way every day, but we do it, just the same. And the people who strive to add value daily are the ones who thrive and accomplish great things.

Give yourself some reminders. Ask yourself, "How do my actions help others transform their lives?" and "What do I do well that adds value to the life of another?" The clearer we are about that, the better off we'll be.

If I can develop and strengthen my Belief in myself, my teammates, my organization and my value to others, that Belief will serve as a powerful tool to help me progress toward my vision. People with strong Belief go farther and faster, and enjoy themselves more along the way.

Making Belief Personal

I'll leave you with three questions to help bring the Pillar of Belief to life.

1. Of the four areas of Belief, where am I strong and where do I need to grow?

2. What can I do right now to build my Belief in the area that needs the most work?

3. How can I transfer my Belief *in* others *to* others today?

Remember:

My only relief from the thief is my Belief.

In the End ...

We've talked about many things in these pages, exploring the choices we make and the paths we take. In the end, what do we have? We have an idea, a practical tool, called The Question Behind the Question, or The QBQ. It's an effective way to ask better questions and make better choices in the moment.

The QBQ is also an idea that works. I know it works because of the changes I've seen in my own life. The QBQ has been the key to unlocking more of my potential, improving my relationships and getting more out of my life in general.

But what about the others we've discussed: Stephanie the receptionist, Jacob the server, Judy the cashier, Steve the manufacturing manager, Patti the brave snake handler, Ted the CEO, Jean, Bob, Craig, Tana and John the sales professionals, and so many more—what about them? Has using these kinds of practical ideas changed their lives for the better? I believe so. And based on my experiences working with individuals and groups all around the country, I truly believe these ideas will work for you and your organization, too.

The QBQ, of course, is only a tool—a method for continuing on a journey that involves eliminating the unhealthy patterns of Blame, Procrastination and Victim Thinking from our organizations and our lives. We've called that journey the path of Personal Accountability. Every word of this book has been intended to communicate what our lives and our world can be like when we choose this path. So let's end our exploration together by looking at three ordinary people whose stories illustrate the power of the master principle, Personal Accountability.

These aren't people who made the big sale, saved the organization from the brink of bankruptcy or performed feats of heroic customer service. They are just good people like you and me who are making a positive difference, every day.

No Victim Thinking Here

In 1959 Carlton Orr was 20 years old, strong and handsome, and had his whole life ahead of him. He was a muscular farm kid from Greene, New York, a rural community where family is important, athletics are a passion and cows are both income and hobby. Carlton wrestled at Cornell University for my father, but only for a year. He was fun to have on the team and showed promise, talent and desire. He always had a positive attitude and was kind to others.

In 1959 Carlton proudly trucked his cows to the county fair, and there he noticed he wasn't feeling well. Inconveniently, he had caught a cold; sadly, he went home ill; tragically, it was actually a deadly disease—polio. Carlton was one of the last few who had not been vaccinated. The doctors gave him about a year to live. I was a year old when he contracted the disease.

Carlton had a great impact on my life. In the early days of his disease, he attended Cornell wrestling meets to support his former team. He was paralyzed from the neck down, so he watched from a wheelchair, breathing with the help of a respirator attached to a tube leading to his mouth. No yelling and screaming at the ref for Carlton. But you could see the Belief and enthusiasm in his eyes.

Every once in a while, out of the blue, my dad would say, "Let's go visit Carlton," and we'd all pile into the pickup truck and drive 10 country miles to the downtown Ithaca nursing home, with me in the back, anticipating an experience. As a young child, I thought it was pretty cool to see his bed that went up and down like a rocking chair. The motion helped him breathe by enabling his lungs to function more easily.

As time wore on, Carlton would sometimes be in an iron lung instead of in the rocking bed. Have you ever seen one of those? He'd lie on his back, completely enclosed from the neck down in a long, metal, cylinder-shaped mechanical housing. The machine helped him breathe by virtually squeezing his body with air pressure to help him exhale, then releasing it so he could inhale. We could hear the constant grinding and whooshing as the iron lung did its critical job for Carlton's body. To me this was eerie.

Carlton had to view us upside-down when we talked with him. That is, he'd look into a mirror positioned above his head and view us backward. The whole setting seemed out of this world and unnatural. But as alien as the trappings were, it was still Carlton in there. And what an impression he made on this young boy.

As he gulped for air, struggling for every breath, he'd say things such as, "How are you today, Johnny?" and "Beautiful outside, isn't it, Jimmy?" Then he'd crack a joke. At some point he'd direct our attention to the wall where yet another card, usually a funny one, had come in the mail and been placed among the others by the nursing staff who loved him so. He wasn't hard to love—not at all—for Carlton was an experience. He had an amazing strength of spirit, and I am a better person today for having known him.

Carlton passed away in 1979. He stayed with us, adding value to our lives, a lot longer than any doctor predicted. If he were here today I would tell him all about the QBQ, not because he *needed* it, but because he *modeled* it. He never played the "poor me" game. There was no Victim Thinking in his world. He never asked, "Why is this happening to me?" There are days I need to think more like Carlton.

No Procrastination Here

My wife, Karen, was driving down a busy four-lane highway one afternoon in October 1994 with a van-load of kids—our four and two of their friends. Suddenly, her eight-cylinder van stalled and Karen quickly pulled over to the left side of the highway. She got the van as tight as she could up against the left guardrail, but there was a narrow shoulder on that side, so most of her "Monster Truck," as I liked to call it, was still sticking out into the inside lane—the fast lane.

It was a busy time of day, and cars were whizzing past her, forced to swerve and swing out of the way to get around the van. "Pandemonium and confusion reigned," she later told me. Finally, she found a piece of cardboard and a black marker. She wrote, "Help! Call 911," on the cardboard and flashed it at motorists going the opposite direction. After about 20 minutes, a state patrol car arrived to help out.

The story behind the story, though, is that in the early minutes, while Karen was searching for paper and pen, Mike, who was barely six at the time, opened the van door to get out. That's right, get out! And that van didn't have sliding doors as do mini-vans; the doors swung outward. So Michael pushed the door right out, probably almost three feet, into fast-moving vehicles whose drivers were using car phones, changing radio stations and balancing coffee cups on their knees.

Now, let me ask you this question: If you had been Karen that day, would you have looked over at Michael and said, "When is he going to stop doing that?" "When is someone going to get him back inside?" or "When will he see how dangerous that can be?" Would you have been sitting back and doing nothing? Of course not, and neither was Karen.

With the speed of a gazelle and the strength of a lion she reached back to her right and, just before Mike left the van forever, grabbed his little left biceps and yanked him back in. There was no hesitation on her part, no Procrastination. She did it in a heartbeat! He had a bruise on his arm for a week, but that was not a big deal compared with what could've been.

Yes, Karen took action.

Of course, why wouldn't she have acted? In that small chance in time we call a moment, the consequences of Procrastination were immediate and obvious.

When we choose Procrastination over action at work and at home, the consequences are not always so immediate *or* so obvious. Whether we're aware of them or not, though, they are coming toward us at high speed: Goals don't get achieved, relationships suffer, issues don't get resolved, problems fester.

Only through action can we protect ourselves and the people around us from those consequences. And when we do, we add value—to their lives and ours. Karen didn't just add value to *Mike's* life, she added value to all who know and love him by protecting him from disaster. Our moments of choice may be less dramatic, yet each day we bring value to the lives of those around us, and to our own—but only when we avoid Procrastination and take action.

No Blame Here

Suzy Wurtz is a leader at the Young America Corporation. She heard about the QBQ on a Thursday morning when I spoke at their annual sales meeting. On Monday, I received an e-mail from her. This is what it said:

> From: Suzy
>
> To: John
>
> Subject: Your QBQ Presentation
>
> John,
>
> I got home late on Friday (around 7 p.m.) after a 40-mile commute. I was dog-tired. My husband was already home. I walked into the house and this is what I saw: children bouncing on our brand new couch, dinner not yet started and everything in a complete mess. There were some things I wanted to say to my husband, but I don't believe they would have gone over well.
>
> I stopped and thought about the QBQ and I knew there was a better choice for me to make. So I looked at my

husband and said, "Honey, what can I do right now to lighten your burden?" Well, after he picked up his jaw from the floor, he looked at me and said, "Who the heck are you and what have you done with my wife?"

Thanks, John. The QBQ really works!

Suzy

I chuckle every time I think of her husband's response. Yet it's Suzy's response to the situation before her that is really exciting. In a difficult moment, she chose the path of Personal Accountability. What else could she have done? Blamed? Definitely. IQs could have come freely, such as, "Who made this mess?" "Who is going to clean this place up?" and "Who'll start helping me out for a change?"

In those everyday moments when I want to find fault, I think of Suzy. She's a model for all of us to follow. It's great to find a person hungry to help and not bursting with Blame.

Whether it's Carlton's outlook, Karen's action or Suzy's not falling prey to the Blame Game, each of us can take lessons from these and all the others we've talked about, and apply them to our own lives. We can come away better people and reap more of the rewards life has to offer.

It's as Simple as That

I'm so glad you've taken this journey with me on the path of Personal Accountability. I want to close by encouraging each of us again to take action. Let's eliminate from our lives today the "Why" questions that lead us down the low road of Victim Thinking, the "When" questions that align us with the Friend of Failure, Procrastination, and the "Who" questions that lead us into the pit of Blame! Instead, let's ask

QBQs, questions that begin with "What" or "How," contain an "I" and focus on action.

When you and I look at our organizations and our lives, if we can just take a moment and ask ourselves the QBQs, "What can I do to make a difference?" and "How can I contribute today?" I know we'll each discover, as so many have, the amazing difference Personal Accountability makes. That's what this book is all about.

It's as simple as that.

The award winning training film

"Personal Accountability and the QBQ"

is now available to you and your organization.

This 18 minute video, along with a comprehensive facilitator's manual, is an excellent and practical resource for all those who understand the power of Personal Accountability.

A story-based module featuring John Miller, this fast-paced, easy to facilitate learning tool, instructs the three disciplines for creating and practicing The Question Behind the Question (QBQ).

It is ideal for:

- classroom training
- team learning sessions
- off-site retreats
- staff meetings
- one on one coaching
- executive study groups
- large group gatherings

- ## Any individual who wants to learn, change, and grow

To obtain your preview copy, call ChartHouse Learning (producers of Joel Barker's *Business of Paradigms* series) at 1-800-328-3789, or your training film distributor *today!*